GUERRILLA
CREDIT

GUERRILLA CREDIT

Learn the Unconventional Ways to Get Cash for Your Business Today

Jay Conrad Levinson

&

Mike Warren

Foreword by David Fagan

On the Inside Press
Beverly Hills, California

Guerrilla Credit: Learn the Unconventional Ways to Get Cash for Your Business Today

Library of Congress Control Number 2013906941
ISBN 978-0-9857581-4-1

Cover design by Carli Smith.
Edited by Gwendolyn Weiler.

Printed in United States of America.

This book is dedicated to all the struggling entrepreneurs and small business owners who are tired of banks taking advantage of them in a system where the average person is set up to fail. I wrote this book with you in mind because I've been in your shoes and it's time to set the record straight.

- Mike Warren

Table of Contents

FOREWORD

As the former CEO of Guerrilla Marketing I've had to set the record straight and explain many times what Guerrilla Marketing really is. It all starts with the word Guerrilla, which essentially means the unconventional way of reaching conventional goals. Guerrilla Marketing, therefore, is the unconventional way of reaching the common goal of creating and capturing leads that will convert into more sales.

Some people think 'cheap' or 'inexpensive' when they think of guerrilla methods; although that's possible, that's not necessarily the case. Working in a guerrilla way can also mean being creative, hardworking, and cutting edge.

In this very impressive book of Guerrilla Credit, Mike Warren lays out the unconventional, creative, cutting edge, and proven ways to build your business credit. Very few people know how to acquire the money and resources a business owner needs to take advantage of all the opportunities that present themselves. This book does exactly that, and I don't quite know how the banks are going to take that. You see, the big banks that the government supports in more ways than one don't really want you to have the contents of this book, let alone understand and apply the contents of this book. The knowledge you gain in these pages increases your power and decreases theirs.

Having worked at several banks over the course of more than six years during several mergers, I know a little something about banks. I started out in collections and fraud and then moved into the lending arena. By the time I left, I oversaw nine different bank branches as it pertained to lending. I know the way underwriters, loan processors, and brokers think. There is a game that gets played. Unfortunately borrowers don't really know the rules...until now that is.

Of course, I understand some of the bank and the government's concerns. The power that comes from building credit is an awesome responsibility that's not for the faint of heart. I liken it to a shot gun. You can hunt and provide food with it. You can protect your family and have security with it. Yet at the same time you wouldn't give it to a child. You would train people so they didn't shoot themselves in the foot…or worse, kill someone. Although I've never seen credit kill someone, I have seen credit used unwisely and kill someone's business. Fortunately this book covers that too.

The fact of the matter is that we, as business owners, live and work in hallways with lots of opening doors. In order to walk through these doors of opportunity we have to pay first. That payment may take the shape of needed inventory, advertising, marketing, hiring talent, acquiring other companies, office equipment, tools of the trade, work space, etc. When we don't have the money or credit to walk through those doors of opportunity, we lose out on key power plays that might lead to greater profitability. Have you ever had an idea or seen an opportunity that passed you by and went to someone else? How did that make you feel? It's not a good feeling is it?

You don't have to have that feeling anymore! This book is your key to building credit responsibly so that you can afford greater opportunities, level the playing field, and compete more aggressively in the market place!

More and more, so called experts are coming out of the woodwork on this topic, but I believe Mike Warren practices what he preaches. Mike has the integrity and experiences necessary to best qualify him to teach the topics in this book. Between Jay Conrad Levinson and Mike Warren you can't go wrong. As long as you follow their teaching to the letter you will succeed, guaranteed!

Engage!

David T. Fagan
www.DavidTFagan.com
David@DavidTFagan.com

INTRODUCTION

Welcome, my friend. I am very excited to discuss a topic that is important to you for a number of reasons; that topic is business credit. There are a lot of misconceptions and a lot of misinformation out there relating to business credit, which I aim to clear up once and for all in the following pages.

Guerrilla Marketing books, like *Guerrilla Marketing for Dummies* and other related titles, have sold more than 24 million copies worldwide. I am the only person that Guerilla Marketing approached and that they endorse to teach the secrets of business credit because of the way that I do it and the success rate that I have in helping people from all over the world (literally) get cash lines of credit with corporations.

The purpose of this book is to show you guerrilla methods to creatively (and cheaply) get credit and cash for your business. As you know, the Guerrilla Marketing Series is designed for people who want simple, proven ways to market their business without spending tons of cash or wasting lots of time. It gets people fast, predictable results. It uses unconventional, out of the box methods to reach conventional goals.

Getting the process right is especially relevant today because banks and other lending institutions are getting more and more stringent on loaning to small businesses and entrepreneurs. They are rejecting many applications for lines of credit, or business loans from individuals who are trying to build their "dream" business. The denial of these requests is partly due to the economy, but the other problem is due to the applicant not completing their documents correctly or setting up their business entity correctly. The banks won't generally tell you why they rejected you, so you have no idea what you did wrong.

Although you may not be able to do much about the economy, you can definitely make sure you've done everything to cross your T's and dot your I's, which will remove more hurdles than you realize when it comes to getting the credit you're after. There are several key steps that are critical to setting up your business correctly so that when a lending institution runs your business credit report, all the important elements match. Laws and practices may vary from state to state, but this book will give you a solid foundation on which to build, regardless of where you live. In addition to giving you some thorough, basic resources for this, I also give you web addresses to each state's box of resources so that you can dig even deeper.

If you're in business today – regardless of your niche, services, or how you're currently operating – this information is relevant to you. It's in your best interest to pay attention and read through until the very end because I'm going to be covering a lot of good stuff.

Let me just give you a little bit more background about who I am. I am Mike Warren, a serial entrepreneur who has started several multi-million dollar companies because I love the passion of starting something new, building it, and then passing it on to qualified people to run. Basically, I get the benefits of owning a business without actually having to do the day-to-day work.

I have been a real estate investor, business maverick, and author for over two decades. I also happen to have a double MBA, which is especially relevant for this particular topic because one of my MBAs is in finance; so I'm actually someone that "gets" this whole financial world – which is very important when we talk about credit and lines of credit.

I have extensive experience helping business owners build businesses and resolve outstanding credit issues, whether they are personal or business related. I used to run a debt settlement company where I helped folks settle their debts at a 40% to 80% discount. For example, let's say you owed $10,000. A debt settlement could allow that debt to be paid off anywhere from 20 to 60 cents on the dollar – which is huge.

I use my many years of experience to help entrepreneurs and investors gain access to much needed cash – and now I am sharing that with you. Please make sure to read through to the end, as this is packed with great details you do not want to miss. However, I am not an attorney or a CPA. I am not offering legal or accounting advice.

But what I can't wait to offer you is a strategy of suggested, time-tested strategies to build and enhance your business credit without affecting your personal credit rating. The added bonus is that I will show you several additional strategies to improve your personal credit as well. The most exciting part is that I've saved some of my very best strategies – strategies I have, until now, only shared with my inner circle, private students, and some of my Mastermind partners – just for you. Additionally, I will share some other strategies that I've never shared with anyone else.

Being involved with the different businesses that I'm in – I invest in judgments, defaulted paper, real estate, and buying and selling businesses – what I like to do, and the way that I have cash to do it, is to use business lines of credit to buy my assets. I can tap into those on a moment's notice when I find a worthy investment. And because I'm buying those assets at huge discounts, I can guarantee I'll have the cash to do it. Then these assets pay off huge; and when they do, I pay back the line of credit and use the additional capital to reinvest. That's the way that you should do it as well.

Imagine it for a moment: all of a sudden, you are able to get all of your personal debt out of your name, pay your debts off at huge discounts – 40%, 60%, 80% reductions, clean up your credit, and secure hundreds of thousands of dollars in lines of credit that you can access with the stroke of a check and do the business you want to do.

You can start having all sorts of fun and doing the things that you want to in the time that you want to do them. I think that's really critical because that's the point of everything you're doing, right? For me, what I want to do is spend time with my family. I take my son on father-son trips, my daughter on daddy-daughter trips, and then there are family trips where all of us go together. We travel the world.

When you have all of your finances in order, you can have the toys and go and do the things you want to with the people you want to do them with. I say this so that you can understand that business credit is not just a success strategy – it's a life strategy.

My strategies work. They've been proven time and again, and that's why Guerilla Marketing endorsed me.

Knowledge is power, and by reading this book from front to back, you will be equipped with the knowledge you need to get all of the business lines of credit you need. Just take the time to read through this book, following each chapter in order. You will find that I talk and teach in plain English. There will be occasions where I will have to teach you new terms, but I will do it in such a way that it is easy to understand and easy to remember. I guide you every step of the way.

Now it's time to let the learning begin!

CHAPTER 1

WHAT IF?

"Opportunities don't go away; they just go to someone else."

~ Mike Warren

What would you do if you had an extra $50,000 to $500,000 in extra cash at your disposal? Would you grow your existing business? Would you start another one? Would you buy more real estate? Would you do more deals? Well, most people would say, "Yeah, Mike, if I actually had access to the cash."

I know there are a lot of folks out there that can find great deals and worthwhile investments, but they're really scared about going out and getting cash, or they think they couldn't get it even if they tried. The result is that they needlessly miss opportunity when it comes knocking on their front door.

This is where we're really getting into what business credit really is. It's not just a line of credit you can easily dip into in order to grow your business, get more deals, or secure greater assets – it's a door opening into the future that you really want; the one that you know you deserve.

So, why let access to cash be the impassible hurdle to that life? There are a finite number of things to do in order to make it a reality.

I mean, let's be honest. The core of this book isn't really about business credit at all. Sure, I'm going to give you a few definitions and show you the ropes on how to get some serious cash flow into

1

your business. But what it all boils down to – all of it – is *you*, and making your dreams come true.

After all, isn't that the point of business credit? Isn't that the point of your business? The money aspect is just one piece of a bigger puzzle. This might be the piece you are looking at the closest right now, but I'm sure you'll agree that if you stepped back a minute to take in the whole view, you'd recognize (or remember?) that this is all just a vehicle to get you to a specific destination.

I want you to keep this destination in mind as you travel through the pages of this book. Stephen Covey, a renowned leader in the business industry and author of the wildly successful *7 Habits of Highly Effective People* says, "The main thing is to keep the main thing the main thing," and to begin with the end in mind.

So as you handle this piece of the puzzle, remember that it is just a piece; do not confuse getting business credit with your main objective, which is to ultimately have the success you want so you can live the life you want.

Seriously – what would you do if you had an extra $50,000 in cash that you could go out and use for whatever you wanted? What if it was $100,000? Or maybe even $500,000? What would you do? Answering that question will get you closer to seeing this piece of the puzzle in the context of the finished product.

This is why I am going to be talking about a lot of the pieces in this book, and not just business credit alone. There isn't anything you're currently doing in your business that is an island. By that, I mean that everything is so interconnected that I can't really talk about one aspect of it without going into detail about another, and then another. But you can be sure that this is all just part of snapping the necessary pieces into place so that, when it's over, you can step back and have that awesome "A-ha" moment.

Don't Make These Mistakes!

As new or existing business owners, you often get caught up in the daily survival of running a business, keeping the doors open, and making it all work. You may have had some financial success, or maybe you are struggling and gasping for breath as you begin the formation and foundation of your business. Regardless of where you are right now, I want you to be aware of some major mistakes business owners make so that you can avoid them, or correct them.

Mistake #1: Using your personal credit to finance your business.
Mistake #2: Using a personal guarantee, which allows creditors to attack your personal assets.
Mistake #3: Applying for loans without first establishing payment history and a business credit score.
Mistake #4: Not incorporating your business.
Mistake #5: Not being in compliance with the credit bureau requirements.
Mistake #6: Getting red flagged by the business credit bureaus.
Mistake #7: Believing you can repair your business credit.
Mistake #8: Thinking there must be federal laws protecting business owners from the business credit bureaus. (There aren't.)
Mistake #9: Believing you already have great business credit just because you have a business credit card.
Mistake #10: Working with vendors who only report negative payment history.
Mistake #11: Assuming you cannot get business credit because you have poor personal credit.
Mistake #12: Spending years trying to build business credit without help.
Mistake #13: Ruining your personal credit score.
Mistake #14: Not being prepared with proper documentation when seeking financing.
Mistake #15: Not taking action today to establish and build business credit.

Maybe you have already made a couple of these mistakes; I know I did when I was starting out. So let us all hit the **RESET** button and start over, erase the past, unwind the mistakes, and follow the blueprint I'm going to offer you.

In a nutshell, here is what I am going to cover:

- Strategies for creating business goals and achieving business efficiency.

- How to understand the difference between personal and business credit.
- Tips to ensure you get the right kind of credit – without wasting your time.
- How to choose your business name and how to register it with the State.
- How to choose the best legal entity structure for your needs.
- How to choose your place of business.
- How to apply to multiple businesses for credit without hurting your personal credit scores.
- How to avoid the pitfalls that can happen with "personal guarantees."
- How to establish your business credit profile so that lenders come seeking your business.
- How to manage and monitor your business and personal credit reports.
- How to find other no-risk ways to fund your business.
- How to protect and build your personal credit.
- Strategies for healing business and personal credit blemishes and how to take care of problematic debt.
- Resources for cost savings and inexpensive marketing tools for your business.
- Resources for credit repair companies that can boost your chances of being able to use your personal guarantee effectively.

All of these components will get you closer and closer to living the answer to your "What If" question, and to better utilizing your desired business credit as the vehicle you want it to be – to get you where you want to go.

Now for the Straight Talk

I have got to give you just this little disclaimer (this is something that's now required when covering these topics). I am not making any earnings claims. I am not teaching you how to *make* money; I'm teaching you how to *get* money. I also need to reiterate that I'm not an attorney or an accountant, and I'm not providing any legal advice here. What I'm sharing with you is what I have done personally. And I'm sharing stories of what some of our

4

students have done, and how they used business credit to grow their businesses. Of course, seek your own financial accountant or attorney. However, I am confident that as you double check with them, you'll find that the model I'm presenting will pass their test – that it does in fact work.

Not Just Another Credit Card

Enough of that; now let's get to the good stuff. I'm going to give you a plan today that I want you to put into action – actually go out there and use it. Because if you use it, you will start getting lines of credit - $100,000, $200,000, $300,000, even half a million dollars in cash that you could dip into with a stroke of a check. Then you can go on to do the things you want to do – whether that's growing a brick and mortar business, flipping more deals, paying for killer marketing, paying off debts, or any number of other things.

I'm not talking about going out and getting another credit card. That doesn't do it. All that does is create another resource that you're going to use to make a couple of months' worth of payments on some of your other credit cards, and the next thing you know you're in deeper debt. It adds insult to injury, and it's not breaking the patterns that lead you to this place.

What we need to do is break out of that pattern and do something *different*.

When you use business lines of credit, it is a game changer. For some people, having access to five and ten thousand dollars in credit from yet another credit card (woo-hoo!) may make a difference when it comes to covering bills. But I'm not talking about covering bills. I'm talking about changing the way that you do business. And the way that you change yourself and the way you do business, is to secure more cash exclusively for doing the big deals that will bring in the big checks.

All of a sudden, the bills will take care of themselves – you can pay off all those credit cards; you can pay off the car; you can pay off your mortgage. You can do the things you want to – the *way* you want to, *when* you want to, and with *whom* you want to do them with. That's what we're talking about.

Here is the Ugly Reality

Let's talk about some of the challenges that people are facing right now in today's economy. One of the most common questions that I get, especially now, is how do you get cash to grow a business without using your own personal credit. A lot of folks have had to make some uncomfortable financial decisions. Maybe they've had to deal with:

- Declining sales of their business.
- More government regulations.
- Foreclosures of their property.
- Bankruptcy.
- The bank cancelling credit lines without good reason.

The reality today for a lot of people is they feel like they are in a boat, and while it's not quite the Titanic, they're thinking, "Oh my gosh, I'm on a sinking ship that I can't keep afloat." They have the deer-in-the-headlights look, surrounded by credit cards, bills, and other debts that are causing them to drown a little bit at a time.

These are the realities in today's market, and people in these situations obviously feel they don't have access to cash.

Maybe *you* are one of those people.

The Good News

If you're in that kind of a spot, or you know people that are, it's okay. The thing is you actually have access to business credit without having to tap into your personal credit. This is usually news to most people, who believe all they can do is get personal lines of credit in their business name – credit which would be tied to them, or, if they have bad credit, wouldn't even be accessible.

What I'm going to share with you today is a little bit different than that. I am going to be revealing the secrets to unlimited amounts of cash lines of credit, even at 0% interest. This can be done, whether you have bad credit now, or if you have good credit, but too much debt.

If you have everything current but you just have too much debt, you can still get lines of credit. There is a process I am going to guide you through, which anyone can do. I think you're going to get really excited. It is no secret that lots of people are facing financial challenges in this economy. There has been a drastic increase in credit card debt, loan defaults, and judgments.

Heck, even if you were doing well and you have good credit, the credit card companies that were giving you credit before are probably now slashing your limits. For example, you might have had, say, a $10,000 line of credit and a $3,000 balance on that credit card; then you wake up one day and all of a sudden your limit's been slashed to $3,000. It's happened to a lot of people. It even happened to me.

The bottom line is that it doesn't matter what your current credit situation is; this book can help you get $100,000, $300,000, even $500,000 or more in cash lines of credit to use for anything that you want, including eliminating your personal debt. I will cover how to move things out of your own personal name and put them into the name of the business in order to capitalize on tax deductions.

Believe it or not, there are a lot of ways to gain access to cash and build lines of credit that you can tap into at a moment's notice.

> Education is not the filling of a pail, but the lighting of a fire.
>
> - *William Butler Yates*

The Importance of Your Mindset

By now, some of you may be thinking, "Ok, Mike. It all sounds good on paper, but you just don't understand where I am. There really is no hope here. I've sunk too low to be able to climb back out again." I understand that you may have had a situation where something didn't go exactly the way that you expected. Maybe there are even creditors calling you today; your phone could be ringing right now in the next room. You might have a property that's upside down and bills are not being paid.

And you're not alone. A lot of folks have these issues going on because of where our society is today.

But it's very important to be able to compartmentalize those things so that you can focus on still growing your business. Your reality right now is just part of life. This might sound pretty negative at first, but just listen a little longer and let me explain how this is actually good news.

Life is a beast that is constantly changing; it is a complicated machine. When things go wrong, it seems like there is no way out. But the truth is that even though you may be going through some hard times, it doesn't mean the game is over. In fact, you're in the middle of the game right now. By applying a different set of rules, you can hope for a different outcome. This means that while you're dealing with your reality at its most basic level by dealing with the direct effects of it, the nature of life is such that you can also simultaneously be spending energy on creating a different reality altogether – and do so happily.

So, when I talk about compartmentalizing your mentality, I mean that you need to take the negative things that might be happening in your life and set them aside. Acknowledge their presence – don't ignore them – but say, "Okay, I know you're over here. I know the creditors are calling. But you know what? I'm still going to go ahead and grow my business or start a new business. I'm going to make more money because if I make more money, I can take care of this negative issue over here on the other side."

The next thing is to take action. Action is the thing that separates the doers from the wannabes. Everybody wants the view from the top, but you can't reach the summit without making the climb. In the next chapter, we're going to talk about what it takes to reach the top.

CHAPTER 2

NURTURE YOUR BUSINESS, NURTURE YOURSELF

Before we get into the basics of how to build your business credit and get the cash you're looking for, it's important that we lay down some ground rules; we need to talk about setting goals. We're going to be covering some pretty awesome stuff in this book, and the last thing I want you to do is read it, get pumped up, then set it aside and do nothing. That's just not going to work.

As I said in the last chapter, action is the thing that really separates the doers from the wannabes. So, you need to decide now that you're going to put these things into action. And believe it or not, it's not just a matter of resolve. No matter how fired up and excited you get about these tools I'm giving you, they're not going to do you any good without a plan. I don't mean instructions on *how* to use them (I'm going to give you that); I mean a plan on how to execute your success – period.

Building business credit is not the only ingredient to insuring your business success. Business credit gives you enormous opportunities to grow and prosper, but it is important that you also have a great mindset, goals and an execution plan.

Create a Blueprint for Your Goals

The car is packed and you're ready to go – your first ever cross-country trip. From the White Mountains of New Hampshire to the rolling hills of San Francisco, you're going to see it all. You put the car in gear and off you go. First stop, the Baseball Hall of Fame in Cooperstown, New York. A little while into the trip, you need to check the map because you've reached an intersection you're not familiar with. You panic for a moment because you realize you've forgotten your map. But then you say, "The heck with it! I know where I'm going." You take a right, change the radio station, and keep on going. Unfortunately, you never reach your destination.

Map It, Write It Out

Too many of us treat goal setting the same way. We dream about where we want to go, but we don't have a map to get there. What is a map? In essence, the written word. What is the difference between a dream and a goal? Once again, the written word.

But we need to do more than simply scribble down some ideas on a piece of paper. Our goals need to be complete and focused, much like a road map; this is why it is important to talk about goals.

Why is this Important?

Why are goals important? Because without them, you don't go anywhere! And if you don't have a goal, how will you know when you've achieved it? Whenever you see anything worthwhile being done anywhere, it is because someone is behind it with a passion, a belief and a goal. When it comes to your personal life and your business, goal setting makes the difference between mediocrity, and excellence and accomplishment. I often find people *talking* about setting goals, but are they going through the whole process? Typically, the answer is no. By now, you might be asking yourself, "What process?"

What follows is a blueprint for success in goal setting. The seven steps below are a summary of the steps you need to follow. I will cover each step in depth.

Step 1. Develop a DESIRE to achieve the goal.

The desire must be intense. How do you intensify desire? Sit down and write out all the benefits and advantages of achieving your goal. Right now, you can start a list of all the benefits and advantages of getting a large line of business credit in the next three months. Once the list gets between 10 and 20 items long, your goal is unstoppable.

> Life consists in what a man is thinking of all day.
>
> *- Ralph Waldo Emerson*

Have you set personal or business goals and failed to achieve them? I know I have, and I can always point to the reason why they failed. It's because there was not a strong enough desire. Some may argue with that, saying, "But I did have a strong desire and still I didn't get there." Sorry, but the desire was just not strong enough. This section is about *intense* desire. You need to create a passion for your goal.

How do you identify intense desire and passion?

It's what keeps people working all hours – up early, late to bed. It's what fueled Stephen Spielberg from the age of 13 to be a movie director. It's what powered Whoopi Goldberg from childhood out of impossible circumstances to be a very successful actress. The desire dominates your conversation, thinking, and actions. How do you intensify desire? This section will show you how.

Question: Where do desires come from? How do they form?

Unlike animals with their internal programming we call instinct, the human mind has the colossal potential for reasoning, coming to conclusions, thinking things through. So desires start in the mind. Research has shown that impulses are transmitted through electro chemical processes across the synapses, tiny spaces less than one millionth of an inch across, which separate the brain cells or neurons. Patterns and tracks are formed in our thinking processes. Think the same thought regularly and it becomes habit, forming a deep track similar to a well-used path across a field. On the other hand, an occasional thought may pass through the mind and be forgotten, just like a path that is seldom used and quickly becomes overgrown.

Now apply this information to desires

A desire may come into the mind and soon be forgotten in the everyday humdrum of life. But keep thinking about it, keep your mind focused on it, and what happens?

11

The desire becomes strong – very strong. Then? Action follows right after.

So back to our original question – how do you intensify desire?

By listing details, particularly benefits! Like I said, once the list gets past 10 or 20 benefits, your goal becomes unstoppable. Why not do this exercise today with one of your goals you want to accomplish, like following the strategies I'm going to give you for securing business credit? Have you set a goal for your business to make $2,000 to $10,000 this month? Make a list of all the benefits associated with having that kind of money. What difference will it make to your family, your lifestyle, your enjoyment of life, your business growth?

What if one of your goals is to develop a skill or awaken a dormant talent or ability? Write down a huge list of the benefits this will bring you and your loved ones, or your business. The more you write, the more details your mind conjures up, and the greater the intensity of your desire becomes. This is the first step and foundation of achieving your goal. With intense desire fueling your goals, you have every chance of rocketing to success!

Step 2. WRITE your goal down to make it real.

Once it goes into writing, your goal becomes substantial and starts etching itself into your subconscious.

This is such an important part of goal setting. Why is this process of writing things down so important? Also, what is the best way to write down goals for maximum effect?

The easy answer is that writing things down makes them real, as opposed to being just thoughts in your head. Words are an integral part of the thinking process. We can now physically look at it. Words convey images, pictures, feelings, and emotions to the mind. Say to yourself silently "poor" and then follow it quickly with "rich"; you will be aware of the different reactions those words produce in your mind.

Even the act of using the eye in coordination with the hand while holding the pen makes a much firmer impression on our mind as we write out the phrase or expression. Now, when we read and re-read that phrase or sentence, this makes an even deeper and deeper impression.

Here is another important point. When the words are written and then repeatedly re-written, they have maximum impact. Do you remember ever doing something wrong in school and the teacher made you repeatedly write on the chalkboard (during recess, no less) that you will never do "X" again? Why did the teacher make you write it again and again? Because the more you write something down, the more you remember it, and the more embedded it becomes in your mind.

Putting it in writing breathes life into it, making it a force that cannot be easily stopped. To put it simply, "Write Goals Down To Make Them Real."

Step 3. Use DEADLINES As Lifelines!

Analyze where you are now in relation to your goal (where you want to go) and then measure how long you will reasonably need to complete the goal. Then set a date for completion accordingly.

> Karl Kraus (1874-1936), an Austrian satirist, once gave this definition of a journalist: "A writer whose skill is improved by a deadline: the more time he has, the worse he writes."

I am not trying to pick on journalists, but this funny comment does emphasize one thing – a deadline gets results. It creates urgency, it sharpens thinking, it makes things happen. Creating a deadline for you to achieve certain parts of your goals is critical to your success.

Let's take a simple example:

Goal 1: I want to secure $100,000 in business credit.

OR

Goal 2: Six months from today, I will be enjoying greater purchasing power and financial flexibility as a result of having an extra $100,000 of business credit at my disposal.

13

Which goal is more likely to be achieved? Obviously, Goal 2. Why? Because it is clear, has a specific time limit, and a specific expected outcome.

However, it would be a mistake to think deadlines perform miracles. Setting a deadline by saying, "Seven days from now, I will have made an extra 5 clients and $5,000 in residual income," is not going to miraculously deliver success unless you have a strategy and a realistic plan based on your present circumstances.

So, when creating deadlines for your goals:

1. Break them down into manageable stages.
2. Work out a reasonable time frame for the accomplishment of each stage and factor in a safety margin for unexpected delays. This prevents disappointment and discouragement through missing the deadline.
3. Record the deadline date for each stage in your computer planner or diary.
4. Set the deadline date from the last stage. You now have a final deadline date for the accomplishment of that entire goal.

It now has a high chance of being achieved.

You have planned, set reasonable timeframes for each stage, and your focus is clear. What's next? Keep the overall deadline in front of you daily as you accomplish each stage along the way. But most importantly, START.

Step 4. Bypass Resistance and Gather Assistance

As we get into this step, I want you to go ahead and grab a pen and paper (if you haven't already) and get ready to write a few things down. I want you to make two different lists.

1) The obstacles you will need to overcome to get business credit.
2) The help you will need to acquire, e.g. knowledge, people, organizations.

14

If you see roadblocks up ahead on a journey, you take a diversion or try to go around it. No one in his or her right mind would just drive on and hit the obstacle head-on, hoping to get through!

Bypass Resistance

Are there people who don't or can't understand your goal and who discourage you? You will always run into someone who says, "That won't work," or, "It must be illegal," or, "It may work over there, but it won't work here."

These people are happy being where they are. You are reading this book because you want something different. Others will try to pull you down to their level because that is what is comfortable for them. They may not like where they are, but it is familiar and therefore comfortable. For most people, it is easier to stay where they are, doing the things they have always done, than to step out of their comfort zone and do something new.

You have already proven that you are not going to let others hold you back from accomplishing your goals. You have to keep reminding yourself of your goals every day, several times a day. After a while, you stop hearing the people around you. I don't mean that you stop associating with them; I mean that you are able to be with them, but their actions and comments no longer affect you.

Gather Assistance

At the same time, it is important to identify the knowledge you will need to acquire, or the people or organizations that could give you essential help. Research the subject and educate yourself on what you are trying to achieve. I always like to learn as much about a subject as I can. It's important to do this before contacting people or organizations for additional help so that you can ask intelligent questions and get valuable answers and leads. Without knowledge, you don't even know what you need to know to be able to ask!

Then, identify people you know who have accomplished what you are seeking. Talk to them. Get their input on what you are doing. How did they do it? How did they feel once they reached their goal?

So bypass resistance and gather assistance. Including these two elements in your goal setting can make the difference between a failed attempt at the target and a bull's eye.

Step 5. Planning - Looking Ahead To Get Ahead!

Looking back over steps three and four, list all the activities that will be required in order to reach your goal, and prioritize them. Rewrite the list, optimize it and perfect it.

Organizers of a marathon race take time to mark out the course. The path is planned out from start to finish. Otherwise, reaching the finish line would be a matter of chance depending on whether a runner just happened to be in the area to see it! Likewise, achieving your goals requires planning. The time you take to plan your goals will make the end result a lot more rewarding.

In Step three, we saw the need for deadlines and the need to make another list of manageable slices or segments leading toward the main goal.

In Step four, we discussed the importance of bypassing resistance and gathering assistance. You were encouraged to make a list of possible obstacles and yet another list of knowledge, people or organizations that could help you.

Now, Step five involves using all the information gathered from these two previous steps. You need to combine your lists and put the items in a logical order. Lay out the manageable steps in order of progression, inserting the details from your obstacles list and help list.

Get a large sketchpad and play around with the order of things until the plan begins to flow. I like to first get knowledge, then contact people that can help, then outline what I think I can realistically accomplish and how long it will take. I find that I often want to work on the easy steps and keep putting off the harder or boring tasks until later. Somehow, later never seems to arrive.

For instance, reading this book is an essential step to achieving your goal of securing a large line of business credit. But there are

16

several other, hard steps that you need to take in order to make this goal a reality. It's important that you don't just stop after the easy steps; make your list and stick to it.

Step 6. Get a clear MENTAL PICTURE of the goal already accomplished

Make the mental image crystal clear and vivid in the mind's eye. Play that picture over and over in your mind.

Imagine the smiling face of someone close to you; being able to purchase additional assets with the stroke of a check; cashing your first referral check; having your first defaulted mortgage that you bought at a discount pay off just the way you planned. These sentences immediately bring pictures to your mind.

The brain often thinks in pictures. The human eye captures an incredible amount of information with just one glance and relays it all to the brain, which then translates that information into a form we "see." The brain does not need to receive information through the eyes to see every time. It can recall from memory sights, sounds and feelings, and put the whole sequence together and run it like a movie – all inside our head.

Where is all this leading us?

Imagine constructing your own movie, casting yourself in the starring role. Then, act out the scene as if you had achieved your goal – play it over and over in your minds. What would be the result?

Answer: SENSATIONAL!

A movie is made by a lot of people, but a key figure is the director. His/her job is to visualize the script and guide the production crew and actors. So be your own director.

Visualize yourself enjoying the benefits of having reached your goal. This may sound a little off the wall, but many find this technique works. I personally love this part. I visualize myself with all the money I could ever use, spending all my time with my family. Defaulted paper allows me to achieve this goal.

So, what do you do? Try this exercise. In your mind, create your own movie theater. Imagine it now. Imagine the walls, the seats, the stage, the screen. Put yourself in the front row. Sit back, press a button and start the movie. See yourself up there in vivid color enjoying whatever it is you are seeking. Rewind. Play it again!

Every time you want to feel a surge of motivation, mentally slip into your own movie theater and just play your movie again. This mental imaging allows what goes on in our minds to have a direct bearing on our actions, and the results we produce in our lives.

So go ahead! Visualize your goal, create the mental picture and put a movie studio in your head.

Step 7. Be Persistent.

Back your plan with persistence and resolve. The majority of your success depends on your persistence.

In 1915, Ty Cobb set up an amazing baseball record of stealing 96 bases. Seven years later, Max Carey set the second-best record with 51 stolen bases. Was Cobb twice as good as Carey?

Consider this: Cobb made 134 attempts. Carey made 53. So Carey's average was much better. Cobb, however, made 81 more tries and was rewarded with 44 more stolen bases.

So who is really better? Well, Ty Cobb holds the record. In the end that's what matters for baseball players – who holds the record.

When you get behind the big success stories in any given field, you often find the most successful have made more attempts and spent longer hours at the given task than anyone else. In other words, they give the law of averages a chance to work in their favor. They just keep on striking out, often against all odds.

18

Mistakes = Closer to Success

You have to allow yourself to make mistakes with the understanding that you will learn from those mistakes and achieve your goal. Part of the reason you are reading this book is to learn from someone who has made a lot of mistakes. And let me tell you, I have made a bunch. While I am not happy about making a mistake, I also realize I am one step closer to a success.

Yes, the previous six steps are also essential and crucial, *but* – if you do not persist, your wonderful plan can go down the drain. Your vivid mental images can just evaporate into thin air. You must just keep at it day in and day out. Then you are GUARANTEED results – eventually! To maintain this kind of momentum, you have to develop mental toughness.

Mental Toughness

To be mentally tough means you minimize the effects of discouragement and you turn negatives into positives.

For example, when you catch yourself thinking, "This is just not working; this is useless and a waste of time," trigger mental toughness by saying, "Delete that thought!" Instead, think, "What do I need to do to make this work?" Yes, I know old habits are hard to break. Heck, if they were easy, then no one would have any bad habits. It takes time and persistence, but the rewards are worth it.

"The Remaining 90% - Sheer Persistence"

It really does come down to just being persistent. Just keep on going, persist, persist, persist, and let the good old law of averages work for you. You *will* realize that goal.

Now the question is, what goal are you going to set today? What goal can you set for your business, which is going to lift it to new levels? What goals are you going to implement in your personal life, which are going to have a positive effect on you and your loved ones? Take some time now and think about it.

Then?

JUST DO IT!

As a final note on goal setting, take these seven steps and rewrite them on a card or in a notebook for frequent reference. Keep them on your computer in a note on your desktop. Then use the seven steps as a blueprint for success. Keep checking your goal against the seven steps, frequently measuring your progress and keeping yourself on track.

CHAPTER 3

MISSION: CRITICAL

The Big Secret

More money is lent to companies than to real estate investors, homeowners, car owners, and all other borrowers combined. Yet in a review of the top 10 selling business startup books, we found no mention of business credit (aka "trade credit" or "corporate credit").

That's right: not one mention of the single largest source of lending in the entire world!

No wonder startup companies and "little guys" hear about business credit. But the consequence is that they rarely understand how it's established or tracked, or how it affects their lives or businesses. For this reason, credit-building systems will give you a huge competitive advantage, and put you in a league with well-funded companies that make it past the five-year mark with flying colors.

What Exactly is Business Credit?

So, what is this business credit, and how do we get it? Business credit, really simply, is capital or trade credit given to companies for business use. Who determines that business use? You do. You get to decide what it means and how much you're using to run your business. That could be real estate. That could be marketing. That could be travelling to go preview properties or talk to potential clients. It could be getting a new car. It could be paying off other credit card debts. It could be stopping short sales. It could be working on short sales. You name it. The sky is really the limit.

Business credit is also a measure of the worthiness of a business versus its ability to get trade and bank credit. For instance, if you were applying for personal credit, lenders would evaluate you and say, "Yes, Mike, you have the ability to borrow money *and* you can pay it back." Similarly, on the business side of things, they're going to be doing the same evaluation: "Is this a viable business, and does it have the ability to actually pay the money back if we give it cash?" Just remember that there's a way that you need to set things up in order to make it actually work for you and for the companies who want to lend you money.

The Way of the Guerrilla

By now you must realize that being a Guerrilla is all about the unconventional way of reaching conventional goals. This could include creativity and hard work, but it definitely doesn't require a small fortune. It was 1984 when Jay showed his Berkley students, and the rest of the world for that matter, how to market and advertise without a huge budget. Fast-forwarding to today, Jay and his co-authors have been showing businesses ways to level the playing field.

The concept of Guerrilla credit is no different. It may in fact be the discovery of the decade, because now Guerrilla Marketers are learning how to build and leverage business lines of credit.

This means even the little guys can have more capital to invest in their business. This is huge because until recently it was only the organizations with deep pockets and long histories of being around that had the more profitable opportunities. Well, that was the conventional method and way of the world. Nowadays there are strategies that allow people and organizations from all kinds of various backgrounds the opportunity to have money for their business needs.

These needs may include:

1. Marketing and advertising campaigns.
2. Technology for tracking and automation.
3. Payroll.
4. Office, warehouse or retail location.
5. Business travel.

22

Just because Guerrilla Marketers love to save a buck doesn't mean they don't know the value of these things needed to grow a business. I don't think I'm going to have to spend a lot of time convincing you that there are valuable areas of your business that you could benefit from investing some money into – most of which are not hard to get a positive ROI (return on investment) on.

The upside to carefully building business credit is probably starting to sound like a no brainer, but we still need to discuss the flip side of that coin – the downside to using your personal credit for your business.

Even If It's Good, It Can Hurt You

If you're like 92% of small business owners, growing your business is damaging your personal credit score. This happens every time you:

• Apply for business credit with your social security number.
• Run up balances on your credit cards or credit lines.
• Make cash advances.
• Get declined for credit.

Using your personal credit to apply for business loans, leases, or credit lines hurts you in two ways:

1) It can damage your personal credit score. That makes it harder (and more expensive) to get loans, leases, and credit lines.
2) It can keep you from building a positive business credit profile – which is the key to growing your business in the long run.

You Need It More Than You Think

Failing to build a business credit profile can be a quick killer. But right now, let's look at the first consequence. According to our studies over the last 11 years, the typical entrepreneur has 10+ credit inquiries per year. How about you?

Every time you apply for credit using your social security number, another inquiry shows up on your personal credit report, which can lower your score. But that's not all. Every time you're declined, and every time you accumulate debt, your score is affected. Obtaining credit individually and as a business owner all under one credit profile can make it harder and harder to get home loans, car loans, equity lines, and credit cards – if you're approved at all.

Not every business has a business credit profile, which is one reason why some creditors want to check the personal credit information of a small business owner. But if you want to limit your personal liability while running your company, it's best to establish and exclusively use your business credit for running your business. From the perspective of creditors, here are several examples of how they may view your personal credit if used for business purposes:

- You may appear overextended. Businesses require more operating capital than consumers need for daily functions, so your personal credit will not be portrayed accurately if you are using it to run your business.
- Multiple credit inquiries will raise a red flag. To prevent people from becoming overextended, consumer credit keeps track of how many credit or loan applications you make, most of which count against your consumer credit score. On the other hand, business credit does not count numerous applications for financing against you, since businesses usually seek financing on a regular basis as a way to run and grow the business.

Unless you are using the right credit information for the right purpose, you may be putting yourself into a situation where you will be unable to get financing – for your business or yourself – when you need it.

Shotgun Theory

I liken credit to a shotgun, whether it's personal or business credit. Here's why: I can use it to protect my family and even provide food. At the same time, I know better than to put it in the hands of a child. There is a high need for responsibility and for training because there are several pitfalls. Because there are so many pitfalls, because the risk of making mistakes is so great, attempting to build your company's credit without an experienced guide is like crossing a minefield. That's why it's crucial to follow our steps in the right order.

24

Over the past several years, we have time tested our proprietary methods on small businesses, and the result is that they have been able to obtain trade credit, business loans, leases, and other credit lines totaling over $1 billion. However, even with our proven methods, it takes nearly six months of establishing your company's credit worthiness, so if you try doing this on your own and something goes wrong, you not only have to start over and wait another six months, but you could end up falling into the High-Risk category with the credit bureaus. This means they could essentially stop your chances of obtaining any credit in the business name in the future. So it's crucial to both start building your business credit now, and to do it right the first time.

A little known, but easy to accomplish, technique is to use a corporation to build wealth. It's easy to free yourself from any debt problems that you may have by just starting your own corporation. You may feel that starting a corporation is a big scary idea. I want to say first off that you have no reason to worry. It's easy, it's cheap, and anyone can do it, regardless of where you are in life right now.

Success Stories

I often get a lot of questions like "does it really apply to people today, in today's market climate?" My response is yes – it worked in the past, works great today and will work great in the future. As the economy changes, so do the requirements for credit and I am about to reveal these secrets to you. Sounds simple enough, right? It is, and I will cover a lot of secrets in this book for you. In the meantime, let me give you some examples of real people who have made it through the process and whose lives are now changed forever.

And you'll see that they all started their companies with none of their own cash. They were able to bootstrap it.

There was a New Jersey drug manufacturer whose company was only 24 months and one day. He obtained a $50,000 unsecured business line of credit with no collateral, no UCC, and it's Prime + 3%. He got the decision in two days. He didn't need to supply any financials to the bank.

Then there was a Charlotte, North Carolina, business owner who got two different unsecured business credit lines for a total of $250,000. No collateral and no UCC on either one. Both decisions took about a week.

Then there was a doctor in Delaware. He got $200,000 in unsecured business credit in a short period of time. Within the next 30 days, he should end up with between $400,000 and $500,000 with no collateral and no UCCs.

These are just a few people who got the credit lines they needed to grow their business to the next level.

In the words of William Gibson, author of the 1984 book *Neuromancer*, "The future is here. It's just not widely distributed yet."

Nobody has let you in on *this* secret, either

Because your Corporation or LLC is a separate legal entity from you personally, it can have its own credit profile – separate from yours. It can qualify for business loans, leases, and credit lines without harming your personal credit score.

And if you've been held back by poor personal credit – or even bankruptcy – here's fantastic news:

- Your company can get business credit on its own merit.
- Vendors never have to look at your personal credit report.
- You never have to disclose your social security number.
- You never have to provide a personal guarantee.

A Clean Start

The biggest reason to start a corporation is that you get to start with a clean slate without any complications from what you may or may not have done as an individual. Even if you have bad credit right now, you can get a fresh start – a new, 100% legal identity – and be on the road to the wealth you have dreamed about. Forming a new company gives you a brand new, separate, credit history.

Later on, I will talk about personal credit and business credit and how to use them both. I also want you to consider the tax benefits of having a business. As an individual, you can deduct around 150 different items off of your taxes. As a corporation, you can deduct over 350! This alone can save you tens of thousands of dollars on things that you do every year anyway. The only difference is that doing them via your corporation means the US Tax Code allows you to deduct them.

Let's say Mary decides to open a Hair Salon. Mary can use her new business credit to pay for rent, buy supplies like shampoo, scissors, blow dryers and advertising – all of which are tax deductible. And by having access to credit, she can expand her business while others are struggling to make ends meet. Mary then uses her profits to pay off the lines of credit so that she can use them again and grow her business even more.

Other benefits of a corporation

- The interest rates you pay on credit cards as a corporation is generally lower than as an individual.
- The business gets to deduct the interest on credit cards off its taxes.
- When a business buys something (cars, equipment, travel, etc.) it gets to use those assets to make money for the business.
- The IRS says you only have to *try* to make money (profit). It does not say that you *have* to make money with your business. I know lots of business owners who run their business at a loss every year, but live the lifestyle of millionaires because they understand how to do it.

Insurance or Rocket Fuel

I have a few rules:

1. I don't ever want to have to walk into a bank.
2. I don't want to provide any tax records.
3. And I don't want to provide any financials about my company.
4. I also don't want any blooming messy paperwork.

27

I want it nice and simple. Give me access to the cash and away we go. In fact, a couple of things that I love most are "unsecured lines of credit," which means it's not tied to me personally; and "interest only" lines of credit, which means I only have to make interest-only payments, instead of principal and interest. Interest-only payments allow me to dramatically reduce my monthly payment back to the lender.

I like lines of credit that can be opened, but don't need to be used. In other words, I can have them open and sitting there, so I have access to the cash when I need it, but I'm not forced to use it at any time and it's not costing me any money. When I know an opportunity comes around – boom! – I have immediate access to the necessary cash and I can jump on that deal and make the money, *without* having to take out a loan.

Why might you want to have business credit? For starters, it could fund the business like we just talked about. It could fund those hot real estate deals. You could buy inventory for your business, purchase new equipment, and expand your marketing – whatever.

One of the first things you'll want to use it for is to transfer any business debts you're carrying on your personal credit. Most of the time our members or our clients have maxed out their personal credit cards on business expenses. Using your new business line of credit to satisfy those debts is really just moving that business debt where it belongs so that it doesn't pull down and hurt your personal credit scores.

Some of our clients are buying and selling businesses. It's kind of like real estate, where people are buying businesses for basically pennies on the dollar. And remember, when you use unsecured business credit to buy, your assets will never be taken away from you. Let's say that, God forbid, you're not able to make your payments one day. Well, since this is unsecured credit, which means it's not secured by any assets, they are not going to be able to take away your cash-flowing property.

But I have to clarify this point before we go on. I'm not suggesting that anybody do this as a way to avoid paying their bills. On the contrary, if you're not planning on repaying the line of business credit, then stop reading this book right now (seriously – put it down!), because I don't believe in doing that. However, settling your debt at a discount, with the creditor's permission, is a great tactic that I will go over later.

> Patricia, a woman who applied what I am sharing with you, says that my book was a real eye-opener. She had no idea how a business might go about building massive business credit without tapping into personal credit lines. She's now got two DUNS numbers on two of her LLCs and beginning to build trade credit for all her different corporations as well.

Definitions

Trade Credit

There are two types of credit. The first one is called "trade credit." Trade credit is like free money. It's some of the easiest money that's out there you can get, and it starts you down the path of establishing business lines of credit. Now, I'm not talking about trade credit where you go and you sign up for your own personal account someplace. No, that's not it. You need to have some type of corporation first. If you don't have a corporation, start one; they're really cheap to start. I have included some resources to help you in the appendix.

For example, let's say it was something like Home Depot. I know you might be saying "Mike, why do I want a Home Depot card?" If you're a real estate investor, at some point you may be rehabbing houses somewhere. And guess what, that trade line gives you access to buy all of the materials you need in order to do the rehab – the paint, the equipment, the paintbrushes, wood, tile, whatever you need in order to do the rehab on the property. That's essentially free money, and it's some of the easiest lines of credit to get.

Cash Credit

The second type of credit is something that's called "cash credit." Now cash credit is where you can actually stroke a check and get access to the cash, however much cash that you have on your credit line, to use for whatever you might want to use it for. If you want to use it to pay off other credit card debts, it's not a problem. If you want to use it to buy a house or anything you need for your business, not a problem. If you want to use it to do marketing, not a problem. If you want to use it to buy a car, equipment, or computers for your business, not a problem. You can use it for whatever you want because it's *your* business. You determine what the business needs are for your company.

Personal Credit vs. Business Credit

As you can see by now, there is a big difference between business credit and personal credit. If you've ever used a credit card, opened a bank account, or financed a car, you have a consumer credit file. Your consumer credit information is intended to help you find the money you need to run your household. It is not intended to help you run a business. It's time to start thinking about is as a completely different animal than business credit.

Scoring Methods

In personal credit, we have something that's called the FICO score. Most of you have heard of the FICO score, which ranges anywhere from 350 to 850. Your credit score determines things like whether or not you are able to get loans, what your interest rate is going to be, your insurance rates, etc. It's determined by the three major personal credit bureaus:

1. TransUnion
2. Experian
3. Equifax

All of your personal credit is tracked by your social security number. Your FICO score is used primarily by TransUnion; Equifax is using the Beacon 5.0 Scoring Modules; and Experian is using the Fair Isaac Version 2. Because we have three different companies with three different scoring methods, you can end up with three different credit scores. Talk about confusing. Most companies, when looking at your personal credit, take an average of the three to determine your credit score.

And folks, it makes a big difference – a huge difference. So if you're looking at your consumer score, you're not even looking at what the banks are looking at to evaluate your personal credit worthiness. They're calculating the information completely differently. And so being able to look at your different credit reports is the first step in figuring out why your credit score is lower than it should be. It is also the first thing you need to do if you want business credit and you want it fast.

The point of this book is not about credit repair. I'm not trying to help fix your personal credit, but by enabling your personal credit score to float up using some simple tools, covered later in this book, your business credit will build at a faster rate. Even those with devastatingly low credit ratings can improve their personal credit while building strong business credit.

PAYDEX Means Payday

In business credit scoring, you have something that's called a "PAYDEX score." It is similar to the FICO score, but the PAYDEX score goes anywhere from zero to 100. The business credit score also determines essentially the same things as personal credit, except for the credibility is based on a business, not based on you as an individual. It's tracked by 5 major credit bureaus (as well as many others), and it's tracked by an EIN number – or Employer Identification Number. That's similar to a social security number, but it's not tied to you as an individual. Let's break this down just a little bit more, okay?

On the business side, we have really two main credit reporting agencies that are used. (There are actually five agencies, but I am only going to cover the top two. The others can be found in the appendix resource section.) The two big ones are called Dun & Bradstreet, and Corporate Experian.

Uncle D&B

Dun & Bradstreet is the organization that enters your data and determines the credit worthiness of your business. They are a research firm that compiles, and also sells, lists and data of company statistics and preferences. They also compile data that tracks and identifies business and market trends. They identify these trends by using information that businesses enter into their database.

Dun & Bradstreet gives you something that's called a DUNS number or a PAYDEX score. The scoring goes from zero to 100. You should be aiming for a score somewhere between an 80 and 100; that's where you need to be. And once you reach that status, all of a sudden everybody and their brother wants to start lending you money. Now, it's not hard to actually get there, which is the great thing about it. But getting your DUNS number is the most critical step in the business credit process. This is also the place that I see the most mistakes made. You would be so surprised to see how many people do not even know that Dun & Bradstreet exist or what they do.

You can establish that 80 score based off of just five different business credit accounts. For instance, one account could be Home Depot, another one could be Office Depot, and another one could be Staples. Just set up a corporate account wherever you would normally shop for materials. Essentially, it's all about setting up the right types of credit accounts with the right type of lenders. Do it wrong and you are dead in the water. I'm going to go into much more detail about this strategy later in the book, but you're pretty much going to set up some basic accounts, get them started, and all of a sudden you can start using these cash lines of credit. It's very, very easy.

Corporate Experian

Corporate Experian gives you something that's called an Intelliscore. Just like a PAYDEX, Corporate Experian calls theirs the Intelliscore. The scoring is also zero to 100, and you still want an 80+ score. The difference here from personal credit is that it is only based off of two trade numbers, not three distinctly different calculations.

Other Business Credit Agencies

Did you know that there are companies that collect data specifically on businesses? These privately held companies are known as **business credit reporting agencies** and they compile their data into formats called **business credit reports**. They collect data from banks, suppliers, finance companies, business owners; and look at public records such as tax liens, bankruptcies, and judgments.

It's important for you to get your company listed because it can make the process of establishing business credit and financing much easier. Just keep in mind that there are over 25 other business credit bureaus not listed here, some of which are industry specific, such as trucking or construction. You may want to look into getting listed with some of these particular bureaus, depending on the type of industry your business is in.

Here are the Top 10 Business Credit Bureaus you should know:

1. **Dun & Bradstreet (D&B)**
   D&B is the primary business credit reporting agency with over 70 million businesses registered in its database. A business credit file with D&B contains information provided by the business owner and its vendors. D&B issues a PAYDEX score based on payment experiences and a DUNS rating based on financials. Its business credit builder program is a great way for business owners to add trade references to their file in a short period of time.

2. **Equifax Small Business Enterprise**
   Small Business Equifax, one of the three primary consumer credit reporting agencies, also provides business credit evaluations for over 22,000,000 small businesses and corporations.

3. **Experian SmartBusinessReports™**
   Experian Business is another one of the three primary consumer credit reporting agencies that provide business credit evaluations. SmartBusinessReports assigns a business credit score called the Intelliscore.

4. **FDInsight™**
   This is a company that is relatively new to the business credit market. It was originally the second largest credit reporting company in the mortgage broker field. The information on its business files is provided by the business owner or a third party, and then every piece of information is verified by the staff of FDInsight™. They are known to provide the most accurate business credit report in the industry.

5. **Credit.net**

   Credit.net is a division of InfoUSA® that generates credit reports on approximately 15,000,000 businesses. The credit analysis provided by Credit.net relies on four criteria: years in business, number of employees, public records, and stability within the industry. Its business credit score is a grading system from A through C (70-100) and is awarded as an evaluation of the company's credit history.

6. **Accurint® Business**

   This is a new business that is a combination of forces between The Better Business Bureau (BBB) and LexisNexis. Accurint Business is like Business Experian in that it provides public and business profile information, including credit history based on payment patterns of small, medium, and large companies.

7. **ClientChecker**

   This is a business credit n   bureau that started in 2003 and specifically targets small businesses, freelance professionals, and contractors searching for information to help them determine which other businesses they should do business with. Rather than providing a fixed business credit score, ClientChecker compiles information based on feedback from its members.

8. **Paynet**

   Paynet collects real-time loan information from more than 200 leading US lenders. The company's database has a collection of commercial loans and leases. It's the largest proprietary database of long-term debt over a period of 10 years.

9. **Cortera**

   Cortera provides credit information on businesses large and small, but then combines it with ratings from a community of small business owners, who provide feedback both good and bad on these businesses.

10. **ChexSystems**

    This reporting agency is extremely important, as it has to do with your ability to open up a business checking account with a financial institution. ChexSystems is a reporting agency banks use, which is a network comprised of member Financial Institutions that regularly contribute information on mishandled checking and savings accounts to a central location.

Reporting Process

In personal credit, nearly every consumer credit card reports everything, so the good, the bad, and the in between shows on your credit report. In business credit, many creditors only report the missed or late payments. Many creditors may not report at all. You can control this process by working with creditors that report to the business credit agencies and report the entire credit history. Yes, the good stuff shows up there, too. Working with creditors that report to Dun & Bradstreet and Experian Corporate will build your credit quickly – much quicker than personal credit.

Speed of Establishing Favorable Credit Rating

Remember when you were young and were applying for that first credit card or car loan? You probably had to have a co-signer or had a really, really low credit limit. It took months, even years, to see those credit limits increase. And what about that first mortgage? It was probably a bumpy road trying to secure it, and what about all those rejections and credit inquiries during the process? You know all too well that it takes years to establish your personal credit history. But it doesn't take long to destroy it; just one missed month of payments or a personal catastrophe can set you back dramatically.

Done properly, good business credit can be built very quickly. With careful planning, it will remain strong and is not affected by any personal changes in circumstance. I will give you a specific blueprint to follow that will get you on the road to establishing large credit lines quickly. Here's a success story from someone named Scott. He's a wholesaler, which means that he takes houses and he flips them.

> Scott used what we taught him and went out and got $88,000. I think the important part is *how fast he got it* – he did it in two months. Some of you may be saying, "Well, Mike, I want it faster." But you need to understand that it takes a little bit of time because you have to establish a history so that lenders will actually lend you the cash that you want.

In just a little over two months, he had $88,000 in unsecured business credit for his new real estate business. Now, that's pretty good when you have a credit crunch and you're thinking, "Oh my gosh. How am I going to come up with the money to buy and sell houses or grow my business?"

Give Yourself the Gift of Clout

Business credit has more clout. It is just that simple, and let me explain why. Even more so than Experian Corporate, Dun & Bradstreet is considered the highly respected source for the accurate reporting of your businesses history. By having a good credit record with Dun & Bradstreet, creditors will flock to you to lend you money. By building your record with them carefully and strategically, your business credit rating will grow and present opportunities to you.

I see this quite often where many people start to go after cash credit before they have taken the time to understand this step. It is so easy and fast to get done as long as you give Dun & Bradstreet the right information. Learning how to do this the right way will be worth the price of this book alone. Many times I see people hungry for credit, but without following the blueprint I will lay out in the next chapter, they end up setting themselves up for failure from the start. The reason is that they keep applying, and then they start getting turned down for credit just based on the business credit inquiries that are adding up. They don't know that by having a Dun & Bradstreet number it can lead more easily to cash credit. In fact, some lines of credit will ask for a DUNS number on their application. Lending companies frequently ask for this information and may summarily reject an application if it does not have it.

CHAPTER 4

BULLET PROOF BLUEPRINT

The Four C's

Creditors look at a number of factors about a business when evaluating it for credit worthiness.

- **Character** includes factors such as: size, location, number of years in business, business structure, number of employees, history of principals, appetite for sharing information about itself, media coverage, liens, judgments or pending law suits, stock performance, and comments from references.
- **Capacity** assesses the ability of the business to pay its bills (i.e. its cash flow). It also includes the structure of the company's debt – whether secured or unsecured – and the existence of any unused lines of credit.
- **Capital** assesses whether a company has financial resources (obtained from financial records) to repay its creditors.
- **Conditions** consider the external factors surrounding the business under consideration – influences such as market fluctuations, industry growth rate, political/ legislative factors, and currency rates.

Successful businesses that include these factors are not built overnight, but the process of building the foundation by strategically using business credit can be started literally overnight. The phrase "business credit market" refers to the business credit bureaus and all of the vendors/lenders that offer business credit. When your company applies for loans, leases, or lines of credit, the business credit market does hundreds – possibly even thousands – of secret compliance checks to assess your businesses character, capacity, capital, and

37

condition. In other words, they scrutinize your company to see if it meets standard lending requirements. We call them "secret" compliance checks because nobody wants to tell you what's being checked. Nor are there any laws giving you a right to know. That's why so many entrepreneurs get blacklisted without knowing it, or knowing why it's happened.

The Big Eight

I've listed below Eight Core Compliance Steps that you must follow in order to rapidly gain business credit, and we'll discuss them in detail over the next couple of chapters. You may have already achieved a number of these, or perhaps you've only had limited or no success with any of them. Either way, I want you to pay special attention. For you to achieve the best possible success, I want you to follow through on these steps in the order and timing in which they're presented with the exception of Step Eight – Protect and Build Your Personal Credit. You should be working on this throughout the process, as it will boost your results with everything else.

After you've achieved the goals in one step, then, *and only then*, it's time to move on to the next step. Skipping steps or moving ahead without completing the previous one will limit your success or cause unnecessary setbacks.

The Eight Core Compliance Steps are:

1. Business Creation
2. Presence
3. Compliance Assessment
4. Trade Credit
5. Purchases
6. Larger Credit Lines
7. Cash Credit
8. Protect and Build Your Personal Credit

Step One – Business Creation

One of the easiest things that you can do is to go out and create an entity or a structure that allows you to build wealth quickly that is not tied to you personally, and allows you to pass that wealth on to your heirs, to your family members, to charity, etc.

You Can Do It!

Robert Kiyosaki, author of *Rich Dad, Poor Dad*, says the best investment you can make is in yourself. You're doing just that – right now – as you are reading and learning. This book is an important first step to help put you on your path to wealth and freedom. How you invest your time is just as important as how you invest your money.

A little known wealth creation tactic is using a corporation to build wealth. In fact, you can create a corporation that is separate from you and all of your debt problems (if you have any). If you don't have any debt problems, or if you don't have any credit history at all, you can still create a corporation and start a brand new credit history. Corporations aren't just for big companies with lots of money; that's not the case. Anyone can start a corporation – and that includes you.

Tax Advantages are Endless

Now why do you even want to consider forming a corporation or starting a company? Well, you get to start with a clean slate. You get a fresh credit history. You get tons of tax advantages. In fact, there are over 350 applicable tax advantages to having a corporation, as opposed to the 150 available as an individual. So, 150 vs. 350. I'll take the 350.

And guess what? You also have the ability to get $200,000, $300,000, $500,000 – even a million dollars or more – in lines of credit for your corporation. That's extremely difficult to do as an individual, but with a corporation it's surprisingly easy.

Create a New Identity

Part of step one is to create a new identity. I don't mean going out there and getting a new social security number, okay? That's illegal. But we can go out there and we can get a new corporation. A new identity could be as simple as going out there and starting a new corporation. Now if you already have a corporation, great. If you already have it in place, you can use an existing one or you can create a brand new one.

Which Form To Choose For Your Business

Going into business for yourself may be only one of many dreams you have. You may just want to be your own boss. Maybe you want to get the kids through college. Maybe you just want to make more money. Whatever your plans, it's important to consider carefully the form your business will take. The right form is not only a matter of saving money on taxes, but also a matter of accommodating liability issues and family considerations.

Things to think about:

- How will your new business impact your family life?
- What impact would your death have on the continuity of your business?
- How easy is it to transfer your business, or your interest in the business?
- How easy would it be to sell or liquidate the business?
- You should decide which form you'll use before you print any business cards or stationary.
- It is always easier to transition your business into a more complex form than it is to move it back down to a less complex form. (Many of our students start out as a Sole Proprietorship and as their business generates income they convert it to a Limited Liability Corporation.)

In terms of securing business credit, we are most interested in discussing corporations, because they are totally separate from your personal financial liability. We will briefly describe some of the other, less complicated business forms here, but for a more thorough study and comparison of the different types of business formations, please see the appendix.

The business forms are listed in order of least to most complex.

Sole Proprietorship

A sole proprietorship is the simplest form of a business. This means that you are the sole owner – the buck stops there.

Advantages

- Little to no bureaucratic red tape involved.
- Least expensive to set up.
- Taxes: You and the business are the same.
- Business losses will offset gains from other income sources.

Disadvantages

- All responsibility for everything rests on your shoulders
- For liability purposes, you and the company are the same

This is a very important thing to consider. For instance, as the sole proprietor, if you face a reversal of fortune because of ill health or some other unforeseeable circumstance, your creditors will still have rights to your money. If you sell your business assets and still cannot pay your personal assets, such as your home or your car, your personal savings, retirement savings, or all of these things may be in jeopardy.

The same liability applies to your personal assets should someone sue you or your company for any reason. If you lose, all of your personal assets and property could be forfeited.

Partnerships

Partnerships fall between sole proprietorships and corporations (but closer to sole proprietorships) in terms of complexity and governmental regulations. The definition of a partnership, according to The Uniform Partnership Act (which has been adopted by many states), is "an association of two or more persons to carry on as co-owners of a business for profit." Let's take a look at two types of partnerships:

1. General Partnership
2. Limited Partnership

General Partnership

This is where two or more people are decision-making owners in the business.

Advantages

1. The General partnership is pretty simple.
2. You and your partners are equals, sharing equally in the management and the profits.
3. You have the benefit of your partners' financial resources, skills and abilities instead of just your own.
4. No one new can join the partnership without permission of all the partners.
5. You don't need a contract between you and your partners, but one is advisable.

Disadvantages

1. You will also share all financial responsibility – even if one of the partners sign a $500,000 contract on behalf of the company after you gave explicit instructions not to!
2. Your personal assets are still in jeopardy should the company incur liability in any way.
3. Each partner is taxed on his share, whether or not the money was distributed during the year.

Limited Partnership

In this arrangement, there are two kinds of partners, General and Limited. The General Partner has the same advantages and disadvantages as in a General Partnership.

The Limited Partner is more like a stockholder. His liability is limited to his investment in the business. However, this partner cannot be involved in the management of the company. If he does get involved, he loses his immunity from personal liability.

Limited Partnerships are normally formed in conjunction with real estate companies for tax advantages.

Advantages

1. Allows access to additional financing through the limited partners.

2. Can have general partners as well as limited partners, thereby gaining advantages of both forms of business.

Disadvantages

1. There is a lot of additional paperwork involved.
2. The state keeps a very sharp eye on this kind of business.
3. As a general partner, you still have all the disadvantages of a general partnership.

Corporation

This is by far the most complex of all the business structures. Business owners that form corporations do so generally to take advantage of a major benefit of this type of structure: limitation of liability. The downside of having a corporation is the added burden and expense of regulations and red tape, and in some instances, the double taxation that hits a corporation.

Corporations are typically formed under the authority of a state government. If a corporation does business in more than one state, it is subject to federal interstate commerce laws and to the various laws of the states in which it operates.

Takes Some Planning

Creating a corporation isn't as quick and easy as forming a sole proprietorship or partnership. The procedure usually involves taking subscriptions for capital stock and creating a tentative organization. Approval must then be obtained from the Secretary of State in the state in which the corporation will be formed. The approval comes in the form of a charter, which specifies the powers and limitations of the corporation.

In many ways, a corporation is the ideal business form even if your business is very small. Corporations are not necessarily giant companies with offices in many states. They can be tiny companies of one or two people (often referred to as "Closely Held"). Using this business form can be a very smart move on your part.

A Closely Held Corporation does not sell stock like a Public Corporation. It is made up of just a few people (or possibly just yourself alone) who are all involved in the day-to-day running of the business to one degree or another.

Advantages

1. Depending on your state of incorporation, you may have as few as one person in your corporation.
2. Limited liability. The corporation is separate from you.
3. The business continues intact even if the owner dies. Ownership of the company is easily transferred.
4. Fewer rules and regulations.

Disadvantages

1. More paperwork and bureaucracy involved.
2. Personal collateral may still be necessary to get loans.
3. Initial cost of incorporation.

Incorporation fees vary from state to state, however you may always consider incorporating your business in another state, such as Nevada, where the laws favor small businesses. There are many sites on the Internet that can help you form a corporation at the least possible cost. If you don't have Internet access, simply look in the back of the Wall Street Journal or USA Today newspaper.

Be sure to do your homework concerning the requirements of out-of-state corporations doing business in your home state. You may incorporate in Nevada to save yourself some money only to find that you *still* have to register your corporation in your home state.

Corporation Types

C-Corporation, also known as a "C-Corp," is started by filing Articles of Incorporation. This is a highly structured business entity and must comply with very specific rules. There are certain corporate formalities that must be observed. The stockholders, officers and directors must treat the business as an independent legal entity, which includes holding regular scheduled meetings, filing corporate papers with the state, and filing a separate corporate tax return. If your goal is to take your company "public" (IPO) and sell shares, this structure is the form to use to reach that goal. One of the advantages of this entity is the greater number of business deductions available with a C-Corp versus an S-Corp. A disadvantage of a C-Corp is double taxation. If the corporation makes a profit for the year, it is taxed. If the corporation passes the profits onto the stockholders in the form of a dividend, then the stockholders are also taxed.

S-Corporation, also known as an "S-Corp," is started by filing Articles of Incorporation. The stockholders file a specific form with the Internal Revenue Service asking that the corporation be taxed as a sole proprietor or partnership. The number of stockholders in an S-Corp is limited to 75, plus all must be citizens of the United States. The advantage of an S-Corp versus a C-Corp is that the profits and losses flow through to the stockholders on their individual tax returns. Only the stockholders pay taxes, not the corporation. Another advantage is that if losses are incurred, they can be passed through to the individual's personal tax return, therefore offsetting, or possibly reducing, their personal income tax.

Limited Liability Company, also called an "LLC", is a good entity to use for small businesses as well as large because it (1) provides the limited liability protection of a corporation, (2) allows the profits and losses to flow through to the members without double taxation, and (3) offers a flexible management structure and allocation of profits and losses. Like a corporation, an LLC offers protection to the owners because they are shielded from personal liability for the business debts or legal claims made against the LLC. The plaintiff (person suing) can only satisfy a judgment from the assets held in the name of the company. Liability protection is critical in this age of unexpected litigation that can wipe out an individual's lifetime of savings.

Corporate Taxation

Because the subject of corporate taxation is far too complex to deal with here, we'll simply say that a corporation is taxed differently than a partnership or a sole proprietorship because the corporate entity itself is taxed on corporate income, and then the shareholders are taxed on the income they receive from their shares in the corporation. In the sole proprietorship and the partnership, the business entities themselves are not taxed.

You can own a corporation and have the corporation hire you as an employee to manage it. The corporation pays you a wage and provides company-paid benefits, such as health insurance. The wages and benefits are tax deductible to the corporation. You pay taxes on the wages you receive. The corporation pays corporate taxes on the profits that remain after paying you for your wages and benefits.

This situation applies to the regular corporation (C-Corp), but not to the S-Corp. The S-Corp is not taxed as a business entity. Rather, the income or losses pass through to the shareholders, where they are taxed as personal income, just as happens in the Sole Proprietorship and the Partnership.

We recommend using an LLC or S-Corp for your corporate structure to build your business credit the fastest. However, this is not legal or accounting advice; it is crucial that you discuss the formation of your business entity with an attorney or tax advisor to determine the best entity to use for your specific situation. If you have previously formed a corporation, now is the perfect time to review with a professional to confirm that you still are using the best type of entity. If not, make the appropriate changes.

Naming Your Business

Give some thought to this decision. The name of your business is often the first image a potential client has of you. And again, first impressions are lasting impressions. You may want to get some outside input for this. Sit down with your spouse or another relative or colleague and brainstorm. Call up your friends and get their help. A catchy name can help potential clients remember you. It should convey:

- Reliability
- Creativity
- Professional Ability
- Trustworthiness

What You Can "Not" Do

As far as the legalities of your business name, if you are incorporated in any way, you must register a trade name, and it must include the words Corporation, Company or the initials Inc. or LLC. It is prohibited or restricted to use terms such as "medical", "national", "bank", "insurance" or "trust" in your company name.

Most states will reject a name that closely resembles one already on file. You may do a name search on a statewide basis; however, you may wish to obtain the services of an attorney if you want to do a name search on a national level.

> Names like "Bob's Funding" or "Annie Enterprises" don't convey an image of maturity or reliability. Annie sounds friendly, but not too serious. Bob sounds as if he still hasn't made up his mind about what his company does. Names of this type sound as if they're running the business out of the spare bedroom. Even if they are, they need not convey that message in the company name.

Formally Create the Corporation

Your next step is to formally create the corporation with the Secretary of State's office in the state in which you are incorporating. In many cases, the information about the entity can be entered online and the Secretary of State will create the Articles of Incorporation. There is a fee for filing Articles of Incorporation, which varies from state to state. To locate the website for your state's Secretary of State's office, you can do a Google search for "Secretary of State (your state's name)." The Secretary of State's website is also an excellent resource for information related to building and maintaining your business entity.

Physical Location is Key

When you are entering the information about your corporation, be sure to use the physical address where your business is located. This can be your home address. Do not use a P.O. Box or an address that traces back to a mailbox facility such as a UPS store. While it is fine to use a P.O. Box for mailing purposes, part of the compliance checks used by the business credit market it to confirm you have an actual physical office address.

Do It Yourself!

We have also located a do-it-yourself resource, which is exactly what it sounds like. You get to do everything yourself and save a few dollars. It's not complicated and there are software systems available to make sure you do it right. I recommend a program called Incorporation by Socrates. It can set up a C-Corp or an LLC. Just do a Google search for "Incorporation by Socrates." Most of the kits are under $40. You can also find a copy at your local Office Depot or Staples Office Supply center, if you have one near you.

Below is a quick summary of the different types of business entities that we've reviewed:

COMPARISON CHART

Type of Entity	Main Advantages	Main Drawbacks
Sole Proprietorship	Simple and inexpensive to create and operate. Owner reports profit or loss on his or her personal tax return.	Owner personally liable for business debts.
General Partnership	Simple and inexpensive to create and operate. Owner (partners) reports profit or loss on his or her personal tax returns.	Owner (partners) personally liable for business debts.
Limited Partnership	Limited partners have limited personal liability for business debts as long as they don't participate in management. General partners can raise cash without involving outside investors in management of business.	General partners personally liable for business debts. More expensive to create than general partnership. Suitable mainly for companies that invest in real estate.
Regular C-Corporation	Owners have limited personal liability for business debts. Fringe benefits can be deducted as business expense. Owners can split corporate profit among owners and corporation, paying lower overall tax rate.	More expensive to create than partnership or sole proprietorship. Paperwork can seem burdensome to some owners. Separate taxable entity.

48

S-Corporation	Owners have limited personal liability for business debts.	More expensive to create than partnership or sole proprietorship.
	Owners report their share of corporate profit or loss on their personal tax returns.	More paperwork than for a limited liability company which offers similar advantages.
	Owners can use corporate loss to offset income from other sources.	Income must be allocated to owners according to their ownership interests.
		Fringe benefits limited for owners who own more than 2% of shares.
Professional Corporation	Owners have no personal liability for malpractice of other owners.	More expensive to create than partnership or sole proprietorship.
		Paperwork can seem burdensome to some owners.
		All owners must belong to the same profession.
Non-Profit Corporation	Corporation doesn't pay income taxes.	Full tax advantages available only to groups organized for charitable, scientific, educational, literary or religious purposes.
	Contributions to charitable corporations are tax-deductible.	Property transferred to corporation stays there; if corporation ends, property must go to another nonprofit.
	Fringe benefits can be deducted as business expense.	
Limited Liability Company	Combines a corporation's protection from personal liability for business debts and pass-through tax structure of a partnership.	More expensive to create than partnership or sole proprietorship.
	Significantly easier to maintain than a corporation.	State laws for creating LLCs may not reflect latest federal tax changes.
	IRS rules now allow LLCs to choose between being taxed as partnership or corporation.	
Professional Limited Liability Company	Same advantages as a regular limited liability company.	Same as for a regular limited liability company.
	Gives state licensed professionals a way to enjoy those advantages.	Members must all belong to the same profession.
Limited Liability Partnership	Mostly of interest to partners in old line professions such as law, medicine and accounting.	Unlike a LLC or a professional limited liability company, owners (partners) remain personally liable for many types of obligations owed to business creditors, lenders and landlords.
	Owners (partners) aren't personally liable for the malpractice of other partners.	Not available in all states.
	Owners report their share of profit or loss on their personal tax returns.	Often limited to a short list of profession.

Apply for an EIN Number

After you have set up your corporation, you must obtain what's called an EIN Number. This stands for an Employer Identification Number, which is used for tax purposes. Just like on the personal side they use your SSN, or your Social Security Number, on the business side they also have to have some way of tracking your corporation so that you're not lost in the sea of all the other corporations out there. This is done with an EIN Number.

A new corporation will end up getting its own corporate tax I.D. number. Now, it turns out that the corporate tax I.D. number is the same number of digits – nine – that you have for your Social Security number. Some people confuse these two. Getting a corporate tax I.D. number is not getting a new Social Security number. Getting a new Social Security number is illegal and you're not allowed to do that. Getting a new corporation with its own tax I.D. number, which is the business equivalent to a Social Security Number, is 100% legal.

To obtain an EIN number, go to www.irs.gov. You can fill out the information online and have your EIN number in minutes.

Register with Dun & Bradstreet

Your corporate credit history is associated with your tax I.D. number, and your resulting credit score is a totally separate number from anything associated with you. Whereas an individual credit score can go from about 800 to 850, depending upon which company you're using to track the credit history, a credit score for a business typically goes from 80 to 100, and is called a PAYDEX score; 80 or above is considered excellent, and it's actually not hard at all to get within that range. We talked about that in an earlier chapter. Right now, we're just reviewing some of the basics.

Getting your DUNS number can take as little as 24 hours when you file paperwork and pay a fee. Otherwise, it can take you anywhere from a week to 30 days to get it. It is FREE, but Dun & Bradstreet will call you and tell you that they can accelerate the process for a fee. DON'T take them up on it. Go to www.dnb.com to get started. Click on the tab that says "D-U-N-S Number," then scroll down to the "Featured" area, where you will see the link "Get a D&B D-U-N-S Number." Click through to get started.

Dun & Bradstreet will offer you a credit monitoring program. You don't need to buy ANYTHING from them at this time. They will send your number to you within 30 days. We will cover in later sections several actions you can take while you are waiting to receive this information.

Register with Experian

The Experian Business division offers Intelliscoring. This is very similar to the Dun & Bradstreet process. Experian is widely used by creditors, too. Go to www.experian.com/business and register your company.

CHAPTER 5

BEYOND BUSINESS CREATION

Step Two – Presence

Once your business has been properly formed, the next step is to build something that's called a "presence." A presence is part of a compliance step and it's really the foundation of your company. You must build the foundation or you're going to find yourself having to tear it down later and start all over from ground zero, which you don't want. So the "presence" phase involves registering the business with the various credit bureaus and directories where lenders search for your business; you want to make sure that you show up on all of these lists.

In order to create the best presence, here are some of the places you need to register or create accounts for your new company:

1. Business Licensing Agencies
2. Phone Directories
3. Cell Phone Directories
4. Banks
5. Credit Bureaus

Licensing

You need to have a business license in order to do business. The license is a means for the appropriate government agencies to register your company to help assure that your actions are legal and the appropriate taxes are paid. Licensing has the advantage of lending a great deal of credibility to your business. Potential clients will be more likely to trust you and feel comfortable about doing business with you. Don't let this frighten you. Most business licenses are fairly inexpensive. For instance, in Colorado it costs only $8.

Depending on the service or product that your company is going to provide, you may need a specialty license. Examples of services that need special licensing are dentists, doctors, lawyers, financial planners, etc. However, obtaining a simple business license will give you credibility and legitimacy that you would not have otherwise. On a side note, you need to verify if your state requires any licensing for your particular business. Just contact your state corporation commission (Secretary of State, Corporation Division). You can find its the contact number by doing a Google search for "secretary of state in X," where X is the state. If the Google search does not work, call your county's planning and zoning department, local chamber of commerce or small business association. Usually this license is not difficult to obtain.

This is simple, but you want to make sure that you explain your business clearly. You may also need to go to your city hall and ask them what types of licenses are required for your city. You will need to give them a general explanation of your business; no great details needed here. However, if you fail to explain it correctly they are going to want to come to your office and do an inspection. They want to see how many people are coming to your home for appointments; they want to inspect the parking situation, bathrooms, accessibility, etc. So you need to let them know what you are doing. Tell them that you are doing no business at your home (unless you are, in which case you have to tell them). This is not the same thing as *working* from home. For instance, if you have a real estate or an Internet business, you may have a home-office, but you would still tell them that you are not doing business from your home because you have no clients coming to your house.

If you tell them this, they will give you a license – no problem. If you tell them differently, they can hold you up because they want to know what you are doing. I went to the city and was in the process of purchasing a building in which to operate my business, and they wanted diagrams, permits, everything.

There are some states that require you to have a state license, but not a city license. We have had people ask us before, "Well, if I am not doing business in my city, why do I need that license?" If you fail to do this easy step, then you are not in compliance with your state's business requirements. What happens is that, since the phone company or any of these creditors are all tied to the same database, they can see if you are required to have a business license or not. If you are, and you do not have one, they will look at you as if you are not in compliance and therefore not a legitimate business. You can find out everything you need right at your city hall.

Get a Business Phone line and a 411 listing

This is simple. You can just call the phone company and tell the person you're speaking with that you want a business line. Be sure to put it under your business name by using the tax I.D. assigned to your corporation. The phone company may also ask you where your business is incorporated in order to verify it with the Secretary of State.

Be sure to ask the phone company to please list your business in the 411 directories. This is important, because business creditors hire companies to verify these types of things to see if you are really in business. You do not want only an 800 phone number – that is much harder to build credit on. You want it to appear that it is a line that goes directly to an employee at the street address listed in your Articles of Incorporation since, after all, you are in business.

Remember, all your phone lines need to go under the business tax I.D., not your social security number. This also applies to your cell phone as well, which needs to be separate from your landline; and yes, you should have both for your business.

Business Phone Checklist

- Call your local phone provider and tell them that you would like to obtain a business line (not just a landline).
- Tell them to "remote call forward" that number to your cell phone or home phone.
- Make sure your new business number has the same area code as the city in which your corporation is located.
- When calling, make sure that you have your corporate charter and tax I.D. on hand. Some companies may ask for that information over the phone.
- Make sure your representative lists your corporation's physical address and phone number with 411 when they set up your account.

Cell Phones versus Landlines

Many people these days are using their cell phones for all phone use. When companies that the lenders hire check on your business, they check your phone lines and send a report of their findings back to the lender. The report will state which lines are connected to a cell phone versus a landline. Now, if you are asking for $20,000 in credit, it won't be a big deal. However, down the line, when you want a large amount of credit, it will be. Another challenge that you may run into if you fail to set up a landline is that they may give you a line of credit and then cancel it after pulling your file, since they do not want to be dealing with a business that is mobile and moving around all the time. That leads the lender to think you are more of a sole proprietor than a business. Just by being in a corporation, banks look at you in a whole new light and you are playing in a whole new game. But you've got to play by the rules.

Most people will never use this landline. Here is a shortcut that I use since I am paying for it anyway. I use the call-forwarding feature. What this does is forward the incoming calls from your landline to another phone without revealing that to the caller. By setting different ringtones, it's easy to differentiate between personal and business calls. This way, you can answer the call appropriately. For instance, if it's a personal call, I usually answer, "Hi, this is Mike..."; but if it's a business call, you're going to want to answer with your business name. Sometimes I will even say, "corporate office" after the title of the business. I do this because many lenders will call and not say anything – they're just verifying that you have a landline running into your business.

Switch your Cell Phone to a Business Account

If you have a cell phone that is not under your business name, this is another step that you will want to add to your list. The reason for this is that some phone companies report to Dun & Bradstreet, which can help increase your PAYDEX score (you will learn more about this in the next step). The two main cell phone companies that I know report to Dun & Bradstreet are Verizon and AT&T. AT&T will report with just one line. Verizon can be a little more complicated because it doesn't report to the bureaus unless you have 5 or more lines. This isn't a great deal, unless you need the five lines, because you won't get any benefit other than the business expense write off.

Sprint is another one that does report, but you have to be careful. Sprint will give you up to 10 phones, but if you should slip just one time on a payment, you'll get a negative report to the credit bureaus. However, as long as you are aware of this and stay current, Sprint is really easy to work with when it comes to setting up a corporate account, as well as transferring an existing account into your business name. This is another great strategy to help build your corporation credit file.

As far as I know, the smaller phone companies do not offer this benefit.

Open Business Checking and Savings Accounts

You will want to select a bank that offers the services you want for your corporate bank account. Many banks offer free business checking and other resources for small businesses. Do some research, speak to several local banks, go on the Internet and investigate banks there. All banks have their own advantages. Your goal should also be to build a relationship with the bankers because eventually you will be going to them for a line of credit.

When you open your accounts, you will need to take proof of your EIN (Federal Tax ID) number, a copy of your Articles of Incorporation, a Certificate of Good Standing (obtained from the Secretary of State's office and proves that your business is operating) and your personal identification. The bank may independently verify this information, but this will speed up the process.

Even if you are just starting out, open a savings account or money market account as well. You are often asked if you have these types of accounts on credit applications, and having those helps to build business credit faster.

Make sure the address, phone, and name on the account are an exact match to the information in your Articles of Incorporation.

Register Your Business with Credit Reporting Agencies

We had you register with Dun & Bradstreet in step one, but there are a number of other business credit reporting agencies. We reviewed these in detail in a previous chapter, but here is a summary list. It is a good idea to register with as many of them as possible. We are not suggesting that you pay for monitoring services, but you want to contact them to make sure they have a record of your business. These agencies are:

1. Dun & Bradstreet (D&B)
2. Equifax Small Business Enterprise
3. Experian SmartBusinessReportsTM
4. FDInsight™
5. Credit.net
6. Accurint® Business
7. ClientChecker
8. Paynet
9. Cortera
10. ChexSystems

Step Three - Compliance Assessment

Regroup, Recheck

Now is the time to take a minute and go back over the actions you have taken in steps one and two to make sure your business information is consistent. It is this consistency that lenders review when considering your credit application.

Here is a checklist you can use. Make sure you have…:

1. Researched the proper business structure for your needs and filed corporate Articles of Incorporation.
2. Obtained an EIN number.
3. Registered with Dun & Bradstreet for PAYDEX scoring.
4. Obtained a Dun & Bradstreet number.
5. Registered with Experian for your Intelliscore.
6. Researched and obtained your required business licensing.

7. Set up a business phone line that is a landline at the physical location of your business.
8. Set up a mobile phone line that is billed to the physical location of your business.
9. Set up business checking and savings accounts.
10. Registered the business with other credit reporting agencies.
11. Verified that the phone number, physical address, billing address, name, etc. on every account, license and registration matches EVERYTHING as it's filed in the Articles of Incorporation. **This simple mistake can cost you hundreds of thousands of dollars' worth of credit opportunities.**

It's Top Secret

There are actually over 2,000 different checks that lenders look at when they're checking out your business. Lenders are so secretive about what the factors are, and the factors have variations, and the variations have variations. All of these add up to about 2,000 different checks. Now, it doesn't mean that you have 2,000 different things that you have to set up, but there are certain things that you have to do.

You need to do everything you can to lower the risk level for the creditors. This includes things like having a business license, having a phone line, a physical address, and the other things that we've addressed thus far. Remember, there're over 2,000 checks that a lender can do. So you want to make sure that you take the time at this step and do it right the first time, or you may end up like a whole lot of naïve small business owners out there that get themselves into the no-credit bucket. We don't want you to fall into the no-credit bucket.

Are They Worthy?

Now you might say, "Well, does every supplier report to business credit agencies?" The answer is no. You might be going out there, trying to get access to business lines of credit, and you may even get credit. After all, there are over 500,000 different creditors out there who would be willing to lend you money and help you grow your business. The problem is that there are only 10,000 of them that actually report to the bureaus.

You could have a line of credit with somebody that is doing you absolutely no good because they don't report to the credit bureaus, which doesn't build up your PAYDEX and your Intelliscore. Remember that 80+ number that we need to get to. If it's not building up your PAYDEX score, even though you have access to the line of credit, it's not doing you any good because you can't get any *more* – it's not helping you improve your credit score for the business. You have to be careful of which creditors that you go to. There's a bunch that work, but there's a higher number that don't work and don't do you any good. I will review many of these creditors in this book, and you can always contact my team directly for additional resources.

Step Four – Trade Credit

Step number four is to start applying for what's called "trade credit." This is a two-part process. The credit application process needs to be segmented and broken down into an easy step-by-step process so that you build a strong foundation on which you can build a house of cash. Once you have gone through the steps to attain your DUNS number and have begun to build your PAYDEX, you should start going after 30-day accounts to build history. Here, I am not referring to the big guys like Home Depot just yet. You want to start building credit by getting 30-day accounts that are available to anyone.

Here are just a few websites for some of these kinds of accounts that I use on a regular basis:

- www.NEBS.com
- www.Uline.com
- www.Quill.com
- www.Arco.com (if you are on the west coast)
- www.BPsolutions.com (if you are on the east coast)
- www.FedEx.com
- www.UPS.com
- www.Kinkos.com/*87

Get 30-Day Accounts Today

You want to find companies that offer a 30-day account, like the ones listed above. Once they're open, you'll want to regularly charge things to these accounts, pay them in full, and then ask the creditor to report to Dun & Bradstreet in order to build your credit history. Gas accounts are a great one to do this with, but try to stay away from Mom and Pops places that do not report to Dun; the bigger chains that offer accounts like these are probably already reporting. Some of the big chains such as Shell and Mobil will require a PAYDEX and proof of three open trade lines, while the midsize-companies that are usually regional can help you attain your PAYDEX at a much faster rate. Once you have your PAYDEX, you can then apply for the actual credit cards places like these offer.

Go to the sites I mentioned above and set up a 30-day account, since these are an easy way to help you reach your PAYDEX. They are going to approve you instantly, and most of these accounts are for products and services you will most likely need anyway. For instance, Uline has trashcans and bags; Neb's offers printing; Quill sells office supplies. Just buy something you need for your business so you can have some buying activity. Do this every month until you are getting a PAYDEX. The gas will be easy. Don't spend a ton of money until you get a PAYDEX, which again will take you between four to six months. Just be sure to confirm they are reporting to Dun. Not all of them will report every month, but these reports are what lead to your business showing up on the radar screen over time, and getting you the PAYDEX score you're striving for.

It's Really Cool

The cool thing about using these 30-day accounts is that the bigger companies usually require you to have three or more trade lines in order to apply for their credit cards. If you open just a few of these 30-day lines and get them working for you, you can go after some of the bigger guys and really accelerate this process. The PAYDEX will put you on a whole other tier of access to credit. It is great to get these lines and then apply for a Shell gas card. You can get a card with a line of credit for maybe between $2,000 - $5,000 and charge and keep track of all your gas. Then, you can increase that line and your PAYDEX score in the meantime. This is a nice thing to have, especially with the cost of gas right now.

Another thing that you can use these 30-day accounts for is to accelerate your payment status. What you need to do is call the accounts that you have 30-day status with and see if they would allow you to pay more than your monthly bill. I know FedEx will allow you to do this. Let's say that you place an order online for business cards with www.Quill.com and they bill you $32 for that month. Instead of paying the $32, you pay $300. What they will do, if they allow this, is report you as a "fastpay," since you don't owe them any money, and they will need to record you as having a credit on their books. Many of my students will start with the 30-day accounts and then, once they have their PAYDEX where they want it, do away with them. I did this at the beginning and it was a big mistake. Even once you have a PAYDEX, you can use the net 30-accounts to get fastpay status and bump up your score by a few points, if you need to.

Once you're in compliance, you've built a presence, and you have established some of these easy credit lines, you'll want to start applying for revolving lines of credit with vendors whose clients are businesses just like yours. They could be office supply stores such as Office Depot, Office Max, Staples; computer stores such as Dell, Apple or Best Buy; appliance stores like Home Depot, Lowe's or any large national retail chain that has any product that could be used for business purposes.

Don't Ignore the Details

Now, it's important that you don't ignore this step – trade credit is the single largest source of lending in the world. It's when one business sells their services or products to you on credit terms, like Net 30 or Net 60, which means they'll sell it to you today, but you have 30 or 60 days to pay if off, respectively.

You want to work with companies that don't ask for a personal credit check, or a guarantee, and you also want companies that report to the credit bureaus. As I mentioned earlier, there are about 500,000 companies out there that will extend you credit, but only about 10,000 that fit into the exact category you're looking for. It can take some time and research to find the right companies, but it's well worth the effort. Otherwise, you could be back to having one credit file, which is your personal credit file, and that's not what you want. You don't want that at all.

It's Not Personal, Just Business

When you fill out your application, check the box that allows the creditor to share information about your business with other industry partners. Remember, this is not your personal information being circulated; it is your business information. Doing this will lead to other credit offers from other resources.

Then the next level will be leasing a car under your new corporation. But you will not be going after this until you show that you have a PAYDEX and Experian Intelliscore in the proper range of 80-100 points.

Step Five - Purchases

Step number five is to actually start making purchases using your retail trade credit. This is where responsibility and strategy are key elements to accelerating building your business credit. A misstep here could cost you enormously.

Not a Spending Spree

I'm not saying go out and just buy stuff you don't need. Only buy the things that you need – that you would normally go out and buy anyway. The difference is that you're making your purchases at the right establishments that will actually report to the credit bureaus on your business' behalf. This is so that you can show that you've got a history of buying the things that you want. You're going to buy them anyway, just buy them from the right places. And of course, make sure to pay on time. Not paying on time is going to hurt you, so you don't want to do that. Also, you don't have to make large purchases; even small purchases will achieve the same goals.

It Could Only Cost $1

Use your business credit cards for regular purchases, even if they're small. Think about everything you purchase at groceries stores, department stores, etc. How many of these items could you also purchase at one of the retailers who've given you trade credit? Examples of this are buying cleaning supplies at Home Depot or bottled water from Staples. Be creative, but don't go out and buy things you don't need and won't use. That is just irresponsible in anyone's book. Shop every month, and shop strategically.

30% Rule

Another tip is only use up to 30% of your total credit limit. For example, if you have a $1,000 limit, do not charge any more than $333 on your card. When you are starting this process, it will show that you use credit responsibly. After you have long established your trade credit and other cash credit lines, you can relax this policy; but for the first several months, be very careful.

The Golden Rule

The next golden rule is to pay the credit card on time, in full, every month. You must do this without fail. Doing this will build your business credit quickly. Not doing this can ruin everything. You should follow this rule now and always. It'll go a long way in continuing to grow your credit, and it is just good business practice.

Check That Score!

After you have used the trade credit lines for a couple months, start checking your PAYDEX score to insure that the creditor's you are using are reporting to the credit agencies and are reporting your credit limits and payment history correctly. Also determine the status of your PAYDEX score.

Step Six – Larger Credit Lines

Size Does Matter

Once you've done that, step number six is to start applying for larger credit lines. This is where paying things on time really pays off. Applying for larger credit lines actually helps improve your business' overall picture to other lenders who rely on your business credit compliance, your presence, your trade history, and your score in order to grant you more and higher lines of credit.

It is really simple to do. Contact your existing trade creditors and ask for more credit. You have been extremely diligent about using the card, paying on time and in full every month. You also consented in your initial application that they can send your information to other industry partners. If you've followed all of these guidelines and practices, then your creditors should view you as a solid business and will give you more credit.

The Rule of 43

If you get turned down, don't be discouraged; just re-apply in 43 days. Why? Lending companies dump everything that was disapproved every 42 days. They can't keep it in their records so they just get rid of it; it's like you were never there. I learned this by applying 42 days after and they said you just applied. Then I went back on day 45 and applied and I got it. This is one of my tricks of the trade, simply discovered by trial and error. It is the same thing when it comes to your personal credit. If you try to challenge something before a certain cycle, the potential lender won't like it or you. Go beyond the cycle, and your chances of the lender working with you will improve greatly.

At this point, you're going to start getting letters in the mail that look like this: here's one offering $25,000 in credit; here's another one for 0% interest on a credit loan; and another one for $100,000 in credit that you could apply for – business credit, so it's not tied to you personally, and you'd have access to it in as little as 15 minutes. But you won't get these until you've already gone through Steps 1 through 5. You have to do those steps in the right order for it to work like this.

Continue to monitor your PAYDEX and Intelliscore for accuracy. Remember also that the credit reporting agencies sell their lists to other lenders, and you will continue to get other offers for trade credit.

Check It Out

When you get random unsolicited offers, confirm that they report to credit agencies and which ones they report to. Make sure to jump on the offers from companies who provide full reporting, which will continue to build your PAYDEX and Intelliscores. Be strategic about getting trade lines from companies that do not report. If they offer products you need that other trade creditors do not, that is fine. Just be aware that they will do nothing to improve your business credit.

Step Seven – Cash Credit

Step number seven is to apply for cash credit, which you can do once you've built your business credit score and you've worked on obtaining a good personal credit score. You can apply for different lines of cash credit and utilize any alternative lending sources that might be available. But don't apply for cash credit until you've completed steps one through six. I know some of you want to go out there and start applying right off the bat, but you have to understand that this is a process. If you follow the process, it will work for you. As a matter of fact, I guarantee it will work for you if you follow the process as I've outlined it for you.

Don't You Dare

But if you go and apply for business cash credit right off the bat, you're going to get turned down because you're probably not in compliance, you haven't reduced the lenders' risk, you have little or no credit history, and you haven't built up your foundation. If you haven't set those things into play, they're going to look at you and say, "No, you're not a good risk at all." They'll flag you – not only for them, but for other creditors too, which is going to mess you up entirely. You don't want to do that.

Here's another example, a case study from Jeffrey Snow out in Philadelphia, Pennsylvania. He wrote, "About a year ago I signed up for your credit building service. We were able to get $4,000 and $7,000 from Dell." He bought and paid for products and then applied for some different credit lines. "We got $103,400 in lines of credit, literally within just a month or two." According to Snow, our benefit statement should be, "We build well for our clients with business credit as a tool." I really like that letter.

Go for the Zero

All the credit cards I recommend have 0% interest for the first 6-12 months, but then they jump up. If you do everything right you can still negotiate your interest rate down, but keep in mind that credit cards are just a means to an end. The goal with credit cards is not to provide you with *that* line of credit, as much as it is to make other, more financially beneficial, lines of credit available to you.

In the short term, credit cards will get you on the map as regularly paying your bills and give you some money to work towards getting more favorable lines of credit. In the long term, business lines of credit should always be your end goal – mainly because lines of credit have different interest terms than credit cards. The cost to borrow and the monthly payments are much less with business lines of credit compared to credit cards. If you max out a credit card and it has matured to its maximum interest rate, the payments can be really high. Business lines of credit are by far the best and least expensive money to help you grow your business.

Here's a Thought

One of the strategies that I suggest is that once you have a business line of credit, you can use this cash to pay down personal credit cards with high interest rates. This can easily be justified, considering that, in most cases, those credit cards were being used for business expenses before you had business credit. But now, you can pay these cards down and increase your cash flow by not paying that high interest each month. One of the immediate benefits to doing this is that your credit score will go up and you can then go after more credit.

You Gotta Get These

Here are the top three credit cards that I suggest you look into:

1. CitiBusiness® Card
2. American Express Business Platinum® Card
3. Chase Platinum Business Card

Make a Checklist

You can also visit our website, where we update the links of the credit cards we recommend on a consistent basis. Below is a sample checklist of the types of credit cards you will want to consider. Half of them are supply, half of them are cash. So use this list to track your progress so you don't miss any opportunities and so you can track where you are.

Credit Card Checklist

	YES	NO	HAVE IT	LIMIT
Direct Lease Card	___	___	___	___
Preferred Lease Card	___	___	___	___
Smart Card	___	___	___	___
Express Lease Card	___	___	___	___
Radio Shack (Cell)	___	___	___	___
Verizon Wireless (Cell)	___	___	___	___
Costco (Credit Card)	___	___	___	___
Key Bank (Credit Card/Line of Credit)	___	___	___	___
Sam's Club (Credit Card)	___	___	___	___
Kinko's (Corp. Acct.)	___	___	___	___
JC Penny/Sears (Commercial Acct.)	___	___	___	___
Staples (Bus. Acct.)	___	___	___	___
Comp USA (Bus. Acct.)	___	___	___	___
Office Depot (Bus. Acct)	___	___	___	___

Take a Deep Breath

For just a moment, I want you to step back and reflect on a couple of choices. You can get the $103,000 line of credit the way that we've talked about; you can go out and do this on your own; you can. But keep in mind that there are no laws protecting your business' rights from inaccurate information, which can cripple your ability to be successful. There's a severe lack of information provided by lenders and the government on what they're checking for. No one wants to tell you these secret compliance checks, and remember, there are over 2,000 different ones. So if you're going to go out there and do all of this on your own, you'll definitely want to strictly follow the advice I've outlined in this book.

Research, Research, Research

If you're doing this on your own, I can't over stress the importance of doing your research. It's up to you to research the companies that offer the credit. It's up to you to research the companies that report your trade experiences. Remember, out of the 500,000 out there, only 10,000 of them report. It's also up to you to research the companies that don't require a personal guarantee or a personal credit check. For the average person, this process is going to take somewhere around four or five years to do.

If you get turned down, don't be discouraged; just remember the rule of 43 and try again.

Done For You

The other option is to go the "done for you" route, and find someone that can hold your hand through the whole process – someone that's already familiar with the 10,000 companies that will report, and the best way to ensure your compliance. This way you can bypass the research time and the learning curve. This offers you greater protection to your business rights, and the chances of your being in absolute compliance will go up dramatically. You can contact my team for more information about this option.

CHAPTER 6

TIME TO GET PERSONAL

Step Eight - Protect and Build Personal Credit

Step eight is to pay attention to your personal credit; don't ignore it. While you're working on the first eight steps, it's very important not to ignore your credit. In fact, it is very important to protect and build it at the same time you are doing steps one through eight. Personal credit is one of your most valuable assets and you need to protect it at all times. So that means watching and fixing your personal credit.

Settle and Repair

I will show you some ways to settle your personal debt and take some actions that will help to repair your personal credit. This is discussed in detail in a later chapter, but conceptually you can settle those debts at a 40% to 80% discount. Once those debts are settled, you can use some basic credit repair and actually have all of those marks removed from your personal credit report. And once you have a perfect credit report – when you're in the 750 to 850 FICO score range – you can go out and buy other assets, or buy a new house, or whatever you want.

You may also consider using the business cash credit you have established to settle your debts at a discount. The benefit of doing this is that you have now transferred the debt from the personal side to the business side, which makes it tax deductible, which is very, very powerful.

I will cover some more about debt settlement in a moment. For now, let's focus on your personal credit and protecting it.

Bite The Bullet – Know Where You Stand

The first step is knowing exactly where you stand with your personal creditors, which will show you where you need to go as far as protecting and building your personal credit. Pull credit reports and get your scores from all three personal credit agencies. The three personal credit bureaus are:

1. TransUnion.
   P.O. Box 2000, Chester, PA 19022-2000
   1-800-916-8800
   www.transunion.com
2. Experian
   P.O. Box 2104, Allen, TX 75013
   1-888-397-3742
   www.experian.com
3. Equifax
   P.O. Box 740241, Atlanta, GA 30374
   1-800-685-1111
   www.equifax.com

Identity Theft and Your Personal Credit

Should You Freeze Your Credit Report

Do you have any concerns about someone possibly stealing your identity or using your hard earned credit for their own purposes and leaving you holding the bag and responsible for paying the debt? Sounds scary, doesn't it? I am taking a few minutes to talk to you about this subject because identify theft is one of the largest and fastest growing scams in the world. I am going to show you how to protect your credit and your identity.

Here is what Equifax, one of the three main credit bureaus, says about credit freezes (taken directly from their site):

- **What it is:**
  You may place, temporarily lift or remove a security freeze on your Equifax credit file under state law or the Equifax

voluntary security freeze program. A security freeze is designed to prevent the information in your Equifax credit file from being reported to others, such as credit grantors and other companies, except those exempted by law or those for whom you contacted us and requested that we temporarily lift the security freeze or those that access during a period of time when you requested we temporarily lift the security freeze.

- **Who can request:**
  Only you can request that a security freeze be placed on your Equifax credit file and only you can request that it be removed or temporarily lifted. Additionally, the security freeze will generally remain on your Equifax credit file until: 1) you request that it be removed or 2) you request a temporary lift of the security freeze for a specific party or parties, or specific period of time, as applicable under state law or the Equifax voluntary security freeze program.

- **Need to Plan Ahead:**
  If you choose to place a security freeze on your credit file, be sure to plan ahead for all of your credit applications. Under the laws of some states, it may take up to three business days to process a request to temporarily lift a security freeze. Additionally, you may not be able to request a temporary lift of a security freeze during non-business hours or on weekends.

- **Victim of ID Theft:**
  If you are an ID theft victim you may be eligible for free security freeze services as provided by your state's security freeze law. You will need to provide Equifax in writing an ID theft report or similar documents as required by your state. Please mail all required information to Equifax at
  Equifax Security Freeze
  P.O. Box 105788
  Atlanta, Georgia 30348

- **Submitting Freeze Request by Mail**
  Although some states allow a security freeze to be placed, temporarily lifted, or removed in other ways, in most cases to request that a security freeze be placed or removed on your Equifax credit file, please make your request in writing to us by mail. To determine how to place, temporarily lift or remove a security freeze from your Equifax credit file, see the requirements for your particular state of residence.

71

To submit your security freeze requests via mail, please submit the following personal ID information: your complete name, including any suffix (e.g. Jr., Sr., etc.), complete address, Social Security number and date of birth.

- For the **placement** of a security freeze, provide the above required personal ID information via mail.
- To **temporarily lift** a security freeze, you must submit all of the following along with the required personal ID information:
  - 10 digit personal identification number (PIN)
  - Date range, if your state allows for a date range lift, (e.g. March 15 - March 21) for the temporary lifting of the security freeze, **or**
  - Proper information regarding the third party to receive your credit report (e.g. Sears), if your state allows for a party (ies) lift.
- To **permanently remove** a security freeze, you must submit all of the following along with the required personal ID information:
  - 10 digit personal identification number (PIN)
  - Two (2) forms of identification (e.g. pay stub with address and utility bill)

Please return your required personal ID information along with any additionally required information noted above to:

Equifax Security Freeze
P.O. Box 105788
Atlanta, Georgia 30348

Charges for Security Freezes:

The charges for security freeze requests on your Equifax credit file vary by state. Go to this address to see the fees associated with your state's file freeze law. (www.equifax.com/cs/Satellite/EFX_Content_C1/1174053574643/5-1/5-1_PopupLayout.htm).

Please include payment by check, money order, or major credit card for the appropriate fees. For VISA, MasterCard, Discover or American Express payment, please include your name as it appears on the card, the card number and the expiration date.

Security Freeze Request Confirmation:

Once we place, temporarily lift or remove a security freeze on your Equifax credit file, we will provide you confirmation. Be sure to retain the 10-digit security freeze personal identification number (PIN) provided to you when you place the security freeze, as you will need this to request a temporary lift or removal of your security freeze. If you **lose** your PIN, you may request a new PIN.

Experian/Transunion Security Freezes:

If you want to place a security freeze on your Experian or TransUnion credit files, you will need to contact them directly at:

Experian:

Experian Security Freeze
P.O. Box 9554
Allen, TX 75013

TransUnion

TransUnion Fraud
Victim Assistance
P.O. Box 6790
Fullerton, CA 92834

Credit freezes are one of the most effective tools against ID theft available

Credit freezes allow you to seal your credit reports and use a personal identification number (PIN) that only you know and can use to temporarily "thaw" your credit so that legitimate applications for credit and services can be processed. That added layer of security means that thieves can't establish new credit in your name, even if they are able to obtain your ID.

Freezes have been available for free to victims of ID theft for some years. Recently, all three of the major credit bureaus adopted new rules allowing even non-victims to have access to credit freezes for a small fee. In addition, most states and Puerto Rico have adopted credit freeze-laws for residents of their state.

73

The cost ranges from $3-$10 per person per bureau to freeze a credit report; a couple of states have higher fees. You can see specific information for your state on the websites below.

The cost to thaw your reports for one creditor – or for a specific period of time – range from being free to $10.

When *shouldn't* you freeze your credit?

If your credit reports are accessed often for work or because you create new accounts with various financial institutions on a regular basis, it is not suggested that you freeze your accounts. The costs to continually thaw your reports would be excessive.

Below, you'll find directions and websites to assist you in obtaining your credit freeze or thaw from each bureau:

EQUIFAX CREDIT FREEZE

- Credit freezes may be done online or by certified mail - return receipt requested. (www.freeze.equifax.com/Freeze/jsp/SFF_PersonalIDInfo.jsp)
- Check your state's listing for the exact cost of your credit freeze and to see if there is a reduction in cost if you are a senior citizen. (www.help.equifax.com/app/answers/detail/a_id/75/search/1)
- Request your credit freeze by certified mail using the sample letter below. Please note the attachments you must include.
- If your PIN is late arriving, call 1-888-298-0045. They will ask you for some ID and arrange for your PIN to be sent to you in 4-7 days.
- Unfreeze: Do a temporary thaw of your Equifax credit freeze by snail mail, online or by calling 1-800-272-9281.
- Sample Credit Freeze Letter

Equifax Security Freeze
P.O. Box 105788
Atlanta, GA 30348

Date: _____

Dear Equifax:

    I would like to place a security freeze on my credit file.
My name is:

_____

My current address is:

_____

My date of birth is:_____

My social security number is: _____

Please charge the $_____ fee to the following credit
card:

Name on Card _____

Type - _____ (Visa, MasterCard, Discover, AmEx)

Number - _____

Exp. date - _____ Card ID# - _____
(V/M/D back 3 digits; A front 4 digits)

Yours truly,

Enclosure:

copy of current utility bill

EXPERIAN CREDIT FREEZE

Experian's credit freeze process is **state specific**. You can find the instructions for your state by going here: www.experian.com/consumer /security_freeze.html.

For the sake of an example, here is the exact process for the state of Colorado directly from Experian's website:

Colorado Security Freeze Process

To request a security freeze, log on to www.experian.com/freeze or send all of the following via certified mail to Experian Security Freeze, P.O. Box 9554, Allen, TX 75013: full name, with middle initial and generation, such as JR, SR, II, III, etc.; Social Security number; date of birth (month, day and year); current address and previous addresses for the past two years. If you are a victim of identity theft, please send a copy of a valid investigative or incident report or complaint with a law enforcement agency or the DMV. In addition, enclose one copy of a government issued identification card, such as a driver's license, state or military ID card, etc., **and** one copy of a utility bill, bank or insurance statement, etc., and make sure that each copy is legible (enlarge if necessary), displays your name and current mailing address, and the date of issue (statement dates must be recent). We are unable to accept credit card statements, voided checks, lease agreements, magazine subscriptions or postal service forwarding orders as proof. To protect personal identification information, Experian does not return correspondence sent to us. **Copies** of any documents should be sent, and consumers should always retain their original documents. We will send you a confirmation notice once the security freeze has been added, and you will be given a personal identification number that will be required in order to remove the freeze temporarily (in order to apply for credit or for any transaction that requires that another party access your personal credit report) or permanently.

To temporarily remove a security freeze for a period of time in order to apply for credit or for any transaction that requires that another party access your personal credit report, log on to www.experian.com/freeze or call 1 888 EXPERIAN (1 888 397 3742), then enter your identification information and personal identification number. The fee for temporarily removing a security freeze is $10. There is no fee for victims of identity theft who provide a valid copy of an identity theft report filed with a law enforcement agency. To temporarily remove a security freeze for a specific party, provide your personal identification number to the party you wish to grant access to your report.

To permanently remove a security freeze, log on to www.experian.com/freeze or call 1 888 EXPERIAN (1 888 397 3742). You also may write to us and provide your identification information and PIN. If you write to us, always include all of your personal identification information and proof of your address as specified in this letter. The fee for permanently removing a security freeze is $10. There is no fee for victims of identity theft who provide a valid copy of an identity theft report filed with a law enforcement agency.

If you move to a new address and wish to keep the security freeze on your file, submit one copy of a government issued identification card, such as a driver's license, state or military ID card, etc., **and** one copy of a utility bill, bank or insurance statement, etc., making sure that each copy is legible (enlarge if necessary), displays your name and your new mailing address, and the date of issue (statement dates must be recent).

TRANSUNION CREDIT FREEZE

- Credit freezes may be done online, by phone (1-888-909-8872) or by certified mail - return receipt requested. *(Some users have reported difficulty with the online method. Please try one of the other options if you too experience difficulty.)*
- Check your state's listing for the exact cost of your credit freeze and to see if there is a reduction in cost if you are a senior citizen. (www.consumersunion.org/campaigns/ learn more/003484indiv.html)
- Request your credit freeze by certified mail using the information found on TransUnion's site (www.transunion.com/sites/corporate/personal/fraudIdentity Theft/fraudPrevention/securityFreeze.page) or you can personalize the sample letter at the following website to fit this credit agency: (www.clarkhoward.com/news/news/ personal-finance-credit/equifax-form-letter-request-credit-freeze/nFbY/) Please note the attachments you must include.
- **Unfreeze**: Do a temporary thaw of your TransUnion credit freeze online or by calling 1-888-909-8872. (www.transunion.com/corporate/personal/fraudIdentityTheft /fraudPrevention/securityFreeze.page)

Ordering your credit reports when your credit file is frozen

You can still order your credit reports when your credit is frozen. Follow these instructions, which come from people who have tried these methods, and let us know how these methods work for you by sending us an e-mail.

- TransUnion: call 1-877-322-8228 and follow the voice prompts (there is no mailing address).

- Experian: call-1-877-322-8228 and follow the voice prompts. If that does not work for you, then write for your free credit report to the following address: Experian Credit Report Request for Frozen Report, PO Box 9554, Allen, TX 75040.
- Equifax: call 1-888-298-0045 and follow the voice prompts. If that does not work for you, then write for your free credit report: Equifax Credit Information Services, c/o Request for Report on Frozen Credit Report, PO Box 740241, Atlanta, GA 30374.

Special Notes

- When writing for your free credit report when your report is frozen, remember to include your ID information and your PIN.
- If you want to get your credit score when your credit file is frozen, please note the following: If you're getting a score through www.CreditKarma.com, you must first unfreeze your credit file with TransUnion.
- If you're getting a credit score through www.Quizzle.com, you must first unfreeze your credit file with Experian.
- The credit score most used by lenders is the Equifax FICO score. You can purchase your Equifax FICO score for $7.95 by calling 1-877-SCORE-11.

What can you do if you are a Victim of Identity Theft?

The following items are included in your credit file.

- **Keep a record.** Because recovering from identity theft can be a long and complicated process, it's important to keep a record of all of your communications. Send all letters by certified mail and keep copies. If you think your case might lead to a lawsuit, keep track of how much time you spend dealing with the problem.
- **Call the police.** Report the crime to the police or sheriff's department that has jurisdiction in your case and request a police report. Though the authorities are often unable to assist you, a police report may be necessary to help convince

creditors that someone else has opened an account in your name.

- **Contact the Federal Trade Commission.** Call the FTC's identity theft hotline at 877-438-4338 and file a complaint. The FTC does not resolve individual consumer problems itself, but your complaint may lead to law enforcement action.
- **Check your credit reports.** Get your credit reports from all three nationwide credit reporting agencies and check for inquiries that you do not recognize and any new accounts opened in your name. Because new accounts may take up to six months to show up on the report, continue to monitor your credit reports on a regular basis.
- **Contact one of the three Nationwide Credit Reporting Agencies to place a fraud alert.** Have one of the agencies put a fraud alert on your file, which will aid in preventing new credit accounts from being opened without your express permission. Equifax and the other two credit reporting agencies, Experian and TransUnion, work together so that when you place an alert with one of these agencies, your request is automatically sent to the other two agencies
- **Place a security freeze on your credit files at each of the three Nationwide Credit Reporting Agencies.** You may request a security freeze be placed on your credit files at Equifax, Experian, and TransUnion. You will have to contact each of them individually in order for them to place a security freeze on your credit file.
- **Block or close fraudulent accounts.** Contact the appropriate creditors, banks, phone companies, and utility companies and have them close and discontinue reporting the accounts. You'll probably be liable for only $50 of the fraudulent charges, but different issuers have different policies. Most creditors promptly issue replacement cards with new account numbers.
- **Mail fraud.** If you suspect that someone has changed your address with the post office or used the mail to commit identity theft, notify the U.S. Postal Inspector.
- **Fraud using your Social Security number.** If your Social Security number has been used to commit identity theft, contact the Federal Trade Commission (FTC), which is charged with handling most identity theft complaints, at 1-877-IDTHEFT (1-877-438-4338). To order a copy of your Social

Security Administration earnings and benefits statement so you can check whether someone has used your Social Security number to get a job or to avoid paying taxes, visit www.socialsecurity.gov/statement/.

- **Fraud involving your driver's license number.** If your driver's license number has been used to open accounts or verify checks, contact your state's Dept. of Motor Vehicles.

- **Fraud involving your passport.** Notify the U.S. State Department's Passport Services Department (www.travel.state.gov/passport/passport_1738.html) of the identity theft so that it can intercept anyone ordering a new passport in your name.

- **Fraud involving a business scam.** If the fraud was perpetrated as part of a business scam, contact the National Fraud Information Center at 800-876-7060.

- **Bankruptcy filed using your name.** If someone filed for bankruptcy using your name, write to the U.S. Trustee in the region where the bankruptcy was filed. A listing of the U.S. Trustee Program's Regions can be found at www.usdoj.gov/ust, or in the blue pages of your phone book under U.S. Government: Bankruptcy Administration. Your letter should describe the situation and provide proof of your identity.

Important Contact Information for Victims of Identity Theft

There are a number of services that can help you respond if you have been a victim of identity theft. Below is a list of resources that we have compiled on your behalf.

Federal Trade Commission's Identity Theft Hotline
877/ID-THEFT

Equifax fraud division
800-525-6285
P.O. Box 740250
Atlanta, GA 30374
www.fraudalerts.equifax.com

Experian fraud division

888-397-3742
P.O. Box 1017
Allen, TX 75013

Trans Union fraud division
800-680-7289
P.O. Box 6790
Fullerton, CA 92634

What are my rights when I go to remedy the effects of fraud or identity theft?

You can learn about your rights under the federal Fair Credit Reporting Act (FCRA) and your rights given by the FTC by going to www.equifax.com/cs/Satellite/EFX_Content_C1/1165255680510/5-1/5-1_Layout.htm?packedargs=Locale%3Den_US

How can I remove a fraud alert from my file?

A written request is required to remove a fraud alert on your credit file. You may write to Customer Service at the following address:

Equifax Information Services LLC
PO Box 105069
Atlanta, GA 30348-5069

Be sure to include your name, social security number, current and previous addresses, date of birth, and telephone number.

How do Identity Thieves do it?

First, they steal your personal information by...

- Going through your mail or trash, looking for bank and credit card statements, pre-approved credit offers, and tax information.
- Stealing personal information from your wallet or purse, such as identification, credit, or bankcards.
- Completing change-of-address forms to redirect your mail.

82

- Acquiring personal information you share on unsecured sites on the Internet.
- Buying personal information about you from an inside source; for example, a store employee that gets your information from a credit application or by "skimming" your credit card information when you make a purchase.
- Getting your personnel records at work.
- Being family members, roommates, or close friends that have access to your personal information.

Then they use your personal information by...

- Opening new credit card accounts using your name, date of birth, and Social Security number. When they use the credit cards and don't pay the bills, the delinquency is reported on your credit report.
- Establishing phone or cellular service in your name.
- Opening a bank account in your name and writing bad checks on the account.
- Counterfeiting checks or debit cards, and draining your bank account.
- Buying cars by taking out auto loans in your name.
- Calling your credit card issuer and, pretending to be you, changing the address on the account. Bills get sent to the new address, so you don't realize there's a problem until you check your credit report.
- Filing for bankruptcy using your name to avoid paying debts they've incurred under your name.

Know Your Real Credit Score

What is a credit score?

Your true credit score is a number between 300 and 850 that evaluates your risk as a borrower. There is one source and one source only for your true credit score (aka FICO score) – the Fair Isaac Corporation.

A score between 700 and 759 on the FICO scale is like getting a B+ in school. Anyone with a FICO score of 760-850 is an A student, or what's called "golden," in the industry, which means you're a great credit risk for a lender.

The three main bureaus hate that FICO dominates the credit score market, so they started selling their own impostor score called a VantageScore. This is just one of hundreds of trademarked, proprietary scoring systems that are competing with the FICO score. Unless you're careful, the VantageScore is the one you'll most often be sold in the marketplace. The VantageScore begins at 501 and tops out at 990.

Getting your true credit score

You have a FICO score with each of the three main credit bureaus – Equifax, Experian and TransUnion. Each bureau's score will vary slightly because of differences in the way they compile your information, but they'll all be similar in range. (**The credit score most used by lenders is the Equifax FICO score.**)

Experian no longer permits consumers to purchase their FICO scores, but these scores are still available to businesses that are doing credit checks on you. The Equifax FICO score remains available to consumers; however, it is bundled with other unnecessary items, like credit monitoring and credit reports. The cost of these bundles is high, ranging from roughly $20 to $40 annually, or monthly charges of $13 to $15. (Remember, you can get free access to your credit reports at www.AnnualCreditReport.com.)

Meanwhile, all active duty military personnel can see their real, true FICO score for free online by visiting www.Saveand Invest.org/military.

What Happens To My Credit Score If...?

Sometimes we forget little things, like paying the cable or satellite bill for a month. Sometimes there is something major that happens in our lives like a bankruptcy, divorce, short sale, or even a foreclosure that causes a major hit to our credit. Here's a quick breakdown of the damage both great and small.

Minor damage:

- Missed a payment on *all* of your bills this month? Subtract between 75 - 125 points off your credit score.
- Credit cards maxed out? Take between 20 - 70 points off your credit score.
- Doing a balance transfer? Expect a 15-point drop in your credit score.
- Applying for new credit? Your credit score will temporarily drop around 10 points.

FICO Score Simulator

This website (www.myfico.com/Products/FICOOne/Sample/ Sample ScoreSimulator.aspx) offers these ballpark figures for free online. For more detailed projections involving more variables, purchase this FICO analysis product for $15.95 per bureau.

Catastrophic damage:

- A short sale will lower your credit score by 120-130 points.*
- A foreclosure will drop your score by 140-150 points.*
- Bankruptcy can decimate your credit score by 365 points.*

* Credit goes to syndicated financial writer Kenneth Harney for these numbers, which are compiled based on your VantageScore – not your official FICO score. Your FICO score would likely take a similar hit.

When you do a short sale, the lender agrees to let you sell your property for below market value and walk away with no further obligations. But if you go into foreclosure, the lender has the right to sue you for deficiency, which remains on your credit report for at least seven years. That means you're responsible for whatever financial losses they suffer as a result of the foreclosure. A foreclosure can lead you to bankruptcy, which remains on your file for 10 years.

A question I get asked a lot is how long do negative marks stay on your personal credit report? Accurate negative information generally can be reported for seven years, but there are exceptions:

- Bankruptcy information can be reported for 10 years.
- Information reported because of an application for a job with a salary of more than $20,000 has no time limitation.
- Information reported because of an application for more than $50,000 worth of credit or life insurance has no time limitation.
- Information concerning a lawsuit or a judgment against you can be reported for seven years, or until the statute of limitations runs out, whichever is longer.
- Default information concerning U.S. Government insured or guaranteed student loans can be reported for seven years after certain guarantor actions.

Some other rules to keep in mind:

The length of time a negative mark can stay on your credit report *starts from the time you were late or the late payment went into collection, not from the last time you made a payment on the account.* Some collection agencies update their reporting status on you to keep the account active with the bureaus, to extend the time the account appears on your report.

This is a technique that some creditors use to extend the life of the debt. Your account might be updated to show that it is still not paid, thereby making it appear that the account is still active. You can challenge this! If you do, bureaus will correctly remove the debt when the debt is seven years from origination. In other words, paying a collection account will not keep it on your credit report for a longer period of time, if you are diligent.

Simple ways to improve your credit score:

- **Always pay your bills on time and pay down the total** amount you owe. *(Accounts for 35% of your score.)*
  If you forget all else after reading this guide, remember this! It's the single most important rule for having a good score.
- Keep a low credit utilization rate. *(Accounts for 30% of your score.)*
  Let's say you have a credit card with a $10,000 limit. If you're carrying a balance month-to-month of $3,000, you're only using 30% of the total limit. But if your credit limit is suddenly dropped to $3,000, then suddenly you're using 100% of what's available to you. That's yet another reason to always pay down

credit card debt as quickly as possible. You always want to stay at credit utilization of 30% or less.

- When you pay off a credit card, don't close the account. *(Accounts for 15% of your score.)* Doing so only reduces your available credit and drives your score down. You want to have between four to six lines of credit. Be sure to use them twice a year – even if it's just for a dollar store purchase – and pay them off right away. That will keep them active in your credit mix.

   If you're facing a huge new annual fee on a card that has a zero balance, try "leapfrogging." That's my term for using the 45-day window you have before any new terms of service go into effect to shop around. So once you get notice about a new annual fee, start looking around for other no-fee credit cards. Submit your application and once you get your new no-fee card, then go ahead and shut down the original one that wanted to spring a fee on you.

- Pay a little extra each month. If you have the ability to pay just a little extra on your bills each month, it can increase your credit score as much as 60 points in just 30-90 days. How do I know? I've tested it myself. Here's what I did. I had a car loan payment, and instead of just making the regular monthly payment, I split the payment up into two payments each month and paid $10 more on each payment (an extra $20 per month). This resulted in the credit bureaus seeing that I pay on time and that I pay more than the minimum due each month. It resulted in my credit score increasing 60 points in 45 days. Try it and see what happens.

Removing Late Payments from Your Credit Report

Late payments are pretty easy to remove. With my new program, they have become super easy to remove. You have to understand that when you apply for personal credit, you need to read the fine print on the terms of agreement. The banks make a lot of money by maneuvering what is read in the fine print. Often, you will find that you have signed your rights away. Some of the things that are signed are basically this: they have the right, if you are one or two days late, whatever the policy is, to state you were late 30, 60 , or 90 days because you gave them that right by signing your signature. This is why I always tell people that if you really want to get technical, go to your creditors and tell them you want a copy of the original application and see if you did in fact sign your rights away.

One way that you can use the copy of your agreement against the credit companies is by removing late payments. Let's say for example that you were actually 40 days late. If the fine print states the late payment is reported that you are 30 days late, you may be able to remove this since, technically, you were late, but not within the 30 days as the document states. I have seen people leverage these types of tasks to credit companies, which clear up your credit. One company that I've heard many students have success with is Lexington Law Firm. They can be found at www.budurl.com/beatirs. Another company is the Credit Repair Office, which can be found at www.budurl.com/dwan. Regardless of the cost - some are as low as $39.00 while others charge as much as $5,000 – the quality will be the same.

Conclusion

I know you want good credit. If you have good credit now, then no worries – you can keep your good credit. If your credit needs a little makeover, then following these steps will help improve your score quickly. Even though this books talks about getting lines of credit for your business without using your personal credit, you need to remember that your credit score remains central to getting good rates on insurance, on your mortgage, on future credit and even being accepted for a job offer. A little tender loving care of your credit today will reap huge rewards for you later.

For those of you who are currently struggling with poor credit, and all the stress that brings, we're going to review some serious repair strategies in the next chapter.

CHAPTER 7

GET REAL ABOUT
YOUR FINANCIAL ISSUES

One issue no one wants to face is acknowledging the financial mistakes of the past and taking aggressive action to solve them. By nature, we would just love to pretend they don't exist. But part of nurturing and growing your business and nurturing yourself is resolving the financial stress. This in turn frees you of the limitations it causes and vastly accelerates your business success.

One issue no one wants to face is acknowledging the financial mistakes of the past and taking aggressive action to solve them. By nature, we would just love to pretend they don't exist. But part of nurturing and growing your business and nurturing yourself is resolving the financial stress. This in turn frees you of the limitations it causes and vastly accelerates your business success.

While the focus of this book is building business credit, I also have a theory I call the Business Credit Triad. This is something that I put together a long time ago. The business credit triad actually has three components. I want you to draw this on a sheet of paper some place. You've got business credit lines, you have debt settlement, and you have credit repair or restoration.

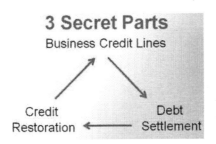

3 Secret Parts
Business Credit Lines

Credit Restoration ← Debt Settlement

Each one of these plays an important role in what I'm talking about. So far, I've been talking about business credit. You can take business credit, and you can use the assets of the business credit to go settle your own debts. Whatever the debt you have, you can settle those debts at a discount. And then we're going to talk about credit repair – I'm going to do that in a second – but let's jump into debt settlement for a second and just talk about what you can really do with that.

Here is a quote by Henry David Perrot. "Wealth is the ability to fully experience life."

I once heard a phrase that went like this: "Being rich is having money. Being wealthy is having time." That's a very telling statement for most people. That is the wish that I actually have for you, so that you can enjoy the time that you get from the money that you have. Having money gives you the ability to do the things you want, the way you want to do them, with the people you want to do them with, in the timeframe that you want to do them.

Eliminate, Eliminate

Let's talk for a minute about eliminating your debt. Eliminating your debt can be very, very simple. In fact, you can eliminate your debt without having to pay anything on it – not a single penny. You could have the entire amount, 100% of it, actually written off where you don't have to pay anything, and you can do this 100% legally.

The debt collectors that are out there, however, do not want you to know this one little secret. It's actually very simple and anybody, including you, can do this. Now some people who may read this book may say, "Oh, well, I already knew that," but they haven't taken the initiative to do it. Other people will say, "Gosh, I never knew that. How come no one ever told me?" That's because these credit card companies don't want you to know that these laws exist to protect you, the consumer.

So what are the techniques? I have many that we're going to be covering in this book, but what's one of the techniques that you can use to totally eliminate your debt right now without having to write or pay a single penny?

The Statute is Ticking

I want to take a minute and talk about something called the statute of limitations on debt. Now imagine for a moment that once upon a time you had some debt on a credit card, a couple thousand dollars, $5,000, $10,000, $50,000, even $100,000. The amount doesn't really matter. Let's just assume that you had this debt. You may be in this current situation right now, or not – it doesn't matter; just imagine anyway. Knowing this secret gives you power. Knowledge is truly power when it comes to dealing with your credit, debts, and how to get rid of these debts.

So, let's assume for a moment that you had this imagined credit card debt, and you did not have the ability to make the payments, so you just stopped paying. Well, the creditors called you for a while, harassed you for a while, and then eventually just wrote it off. But then, all of a sudden, another collector calls you up demanding full payment, plus interest and penalties, years later.

Know Your FDCPA Rights

The next thing you know, that $5,000 debt is now $10,000, even $15,000 in size and they're threatening you with all sorts of different lawsuits and wage garnishment. In other words, they're making all these claims that are often flat out illegal under the Fair Debt Collections Practices Act, or the FDCPA. There are a lot of things they cannot do under that law, like threaten you. Legally, all they can do is tell you that they will pursue the debt in court, which they're fully entitled to do.

However, if the debt has reached it statute of limitations, there isn't anything they can do.

The statute of limitations means that the debt collector has a certain time period from their last demand for payment, or when it was made, to collect the debt. This statute of limitations is usually between two and six years, depending on your state. Look later in this chapter for the statute of limitations on verbal and written contracts, such as a credit card. You'll find this very, very enlightening. You can find this information in the appendix, as well.

91

So let's say you live in a state where the statute of limitations is three years. If the creditor wants to haul you into court on year five, you can go the judge and say, "Judge, the statute of limitations has expired. This is no longer a valid debt." The judge will look at it, see that the statute of limitations has passed, and will then say, "You're right. This is not a valid debt." The case is then marked closed and you're done. You don't have to pay a single penny. The creditor is out because they attempted to collect on this debt after it was written off, and after the statute of limitations had expired.

So under the law, you do not have to pay that debt. That's 100% legal, ethical, and it's a way for you to save yourself literally thousands and thousands of dollars. So that scrupulous debt collector was coming back and saying that you had to pay $5,000, $10,000, even $15,000 in penalties and interest, but all of a sudden that debt is gone and wiped out. They can't pursue you for payment any further.

In fact, if they were to pursue you further, guess what? You could end up having the creditor pay *you* to settle that debt. I'll talk more about that later on.

Right now, let's think about what I just covered. By knowing the statute of limitations for your state, you have the ability to tell the court that this debt is not valid. But let's look at the situation from a different angle now – from *before* you go to court.

Let's assume a debt collector calls you up on a $5,000 debt that's several years old. It's past the statute of limitations. First off, when a debt collector calls you, you should never say that the debt is yours. Even though you think it might be, it's possible that they may be calling you on somebody else's debt. Believe me, it would not be the first time that a debt collector called an innocent person and scared them into paying the debt when they didn't even owe the money in the first place.

Wait a Minute!

So the first thing that you need to do when a debt collector calls you is say, "Please provide me with written proof that this debt is mine because I'm not sure it is." It doesn't matter what other questions the creditor asks you. Don't answer any questions other than providing your name and address so the caller can send you written proof.

Keep in mind, the creditor already has all that information already. So have the written proof sent to you to verify that the debt is in fact yours. Now, the creditor has to do that within 30 days. If it's not done within that timeframe, the debt is no longer collectable. Please note, however, that I'm not giving you legal or accounting advice. I'm just telling you things that I have done, that I've seen my clients do, and it works all across the country, in every single state. It doesn't matter what race, religion, sex, etc. These laws apply to all of us as consumers.

Know the Statute

Let's keep in mind that there's one key sentence here. Paying a debt that is too old – in other words, it's past the statute of limitations – is not required of you at all. You just have to look at your state statute of limitations, or the expiration date of that debt.

Make sure to look at the end of this chapter or in the appendix for the statute of limitations for your state. This allows you the freedom from the stress and the anxiety of worrying about the demanding collection calls because you know you don't have to pay it anymore. The time limit for having to pay that debt is now gone.

Collectors are Not Always Right

I need to point out, however, that there are some creditors who just flat out ignore the law. They depend on you being ignorant of the law and not knowing your rights. So they will call you, they will harass you, they will threaten you, they will do everything they can to squeeze a dollar out of you in order to make you pay. You do not have to put up with that.

The statute of limitations gives you power. That's why the financial lending industry doesn't want you to know what they're up to. If you know their dirty secrets then you'll be able to escape their clutches.

In fact, it's pretty common for a debt collector or a collection agency to call you just before the statute of limitations is about to expire. They'll call you because they know that the time is ticking on their part, and they have to call you quickly. They'll try to threaten you with a lawsuit and all sorts of other things; they'll try to intimidate and harass you into paying on that debt just before it's about to expire.

But don't let fear work against you. Just keep your cool, knowing that you are on the verge of being 100% free of that financial liability.

The Dirty Secret

Here's another dirty little secret that I want to share with you about collection agencies and these debt collectors. Most of these collection agencies will buy these debts from credit card companies. So, let's say the credit card company sold off the debt years ago – typically for somewhere between three and five cents on the dollar. Now, the collection agency is going to call you up and demand sometimes 200, 300 cents on the dollar. For a $5,000 debt, they're adding interest at 29% and 39% for the several years it's been delinquent, and looking for you to pay it all.

So, when you finally agree to settle for just the original $5,000, you think you've eliminated $10,000 of additional debt in penalties and fees, but guess what? They only paid somewhere between $150 and $250 for that particular debt, which means they just made a stellar profit on the deal. That's why these collection companies make so much money, and that's why they're willing to violate the law – because they know the average consumer does not know their rights, and does not read a book like you're reading right now that discloses these secrets.

Now you have the power. You know how to stand your ground, and not have to pay anything.

If you think that's good, just wait until we get into the chapter on how to get debt collectors to *pay you* to settle the debt for zero; that will be a very eye-opening chapter.

Just Keep Your Mouth Shut

Let me just go back and talk about keeping quiet. What I mean by keeping quiet is that you do not admit to owing any alleged debt. So if the collector calls you and says that you owe this debt, and it's showing on your credit report, you shouldn't admit to it. You in fact may owe the debt, but you need to be sure that he's talking about the right creditor at the right time period for the right account. As stated earlier, just ask for the written proof.

One of the reasons that you shouldn't admit that you owe the debt is because it could start the statute of limitations all over again, and now you'll have to wait another five to six years to close it out. This is called re-aging the debt, and is covered more thoroughly later on.

And remember, if in fact you were to still owe the debt, you could use some of the business credit techniques that we're talking about in this book for paying if off at a big, big discount.

Law Firm – So What?

Even if the debt collector says that they're a law firm, don't be intimidated. Don't let them scare you into doing anything. Stand your ground and state that the debt is either beyond the statute of limitations and is not collectable, or, if you're not sure, tell them that you don't know if the debt is yours and to send you written proof.

They Already Wrote You Off

This strategy for eliminating your debt is to simply wait it out. The debt will magically disappear and is no longer enforceable. Keep in mind that the credit card company wrote off your account a long time ago as being uncollectable, which means they got to write it off on their taxes as a loss on their books.

Here's another tactic that you can use when talking to a debt collector: always use the word "alleged." For example, say things like, "Well, you're talking about this alleged debt. Well, tell me more about this alleged debt that you think I owe. So this alleged debt is how much? What was it for? What was purchased with this alleged debt? Send me information on this alleged debt." It's very important to use the word "alleged." This way, you're never admitting that you owe the debt.

The Fair Debt Collections Practices Act has set up guidelines and rules and laws that protect you as the consumer against these unscrupulous creditors and debt collectors.

Re-aging debt

I want to rewind for a minute and make sure that you have a good understanding of the practice of re-aging old debts. The clock on the statute of limitations may start anew if a consumer makes a payment – even a small amount – on a debt that has exceeded, or is approaching the end of, the statute of limitations. Acknowledging an old debt may also extend the time limit on potential debt collection lawsuits. Consumer advocates now advise debtors not to acknowledge old debts, or debts they don't recognize as their own, to avoid inadvertently resetting the clock on the statute of limitations.

"Any new activity on it could re-age it and make it more collectable," says Lauren Saunders, managing attorney for the National Consumer Law Center, a consumer rights group. "You're better off ignoring a call about an ancient debt. It's best to send them a letter (like the one below) saying I don't recognize this or please verify it."

Validation of debt request
(Sent via certified mail)

DATE_____

To: Debt collector_____
Attn: Customer service
Address_____
City, state, ZIP_____

RE:
Your name_____
Address_____
City, state, ZIP_____

Account #_____

To whom it may concern:

This is a written request for validation of the debt referred to in your recent letter. The Federal Trade Commission, in 15 U.SC. 1692g, requires that debt collectors cease collection of a debt until verification of that debt is mailed to consumers.

Please provide this information in writing via U.S. mail at the address listed above.

Sincerely,

Name_____

Print name_____

Statute of Limitations by State

Each state has its own statute of limitations on debt. The statute of limitations varies depending on the type of debt you have – credit card or loan – and is usually between three and six years, but is as high as 10 or 15 years in some states. Before you respond to a collection attempt, find out the debt statute of limitations for your state.

Definitions

- An **oral contract** is an agreement that was made verbally. No contract was written or signed when the agreement was made. Oral contracts are legally binding, but they are harder to prove in court.
- A **written contract** is an agreement made on a printed document that has been signed by both the lender and the borrower. Written contracts are legally binding and easier to enforce than oral contracts.
- A **promissory note** is a written contract that includes a specific promise to pay. The promissory note includes the interest rate, repayment schedule, and consequences of default.
- An **open-ended account** is an account that has a varying, revolving balance. A credit card is an example of an open-ended account.

State	Oral	Written	Promissory	Open
Alabama	6	6	6	3
Alaska	6	6	3	3
Arizona	3	6	6	3
Arkansas	6	6	3	3
California	2	4	4	4
Colorado	6	6	6	6
Connecticut	3	6	6	3
Delaware	3	3	3	4

State			
Florida	4	5	5	4
Georgia	4	6	6	4
Hawaii	6	6	6	6
Idaho	4	5	5	4
Illinois	5	10	10	5
Indiana	6	10	10	6
Iowa	5	10	5	5
Kansas	3	6	5	3
Kentucky	5	15	15	5
Louisiana	10	10	10	3
Maine	6	6	6	6
Maryland	3	3	6	3
Massachusetts	6	6	6	6
Michigan	6	6	6	6
Minnesota	6	6	6	6
Mississippi	3	3	3	3
Missouri	5	10	10	5
Montana	5	8	8	5
Nebraska	4	5	5	4
Nevada	4	6	3	4
New Hampshire	3	3	6	3
New Jersey	6	6	6	6
New Mexico	4	6	6	4
New York	6	6	6	6
North Carolina	3	3	5	3
North Dakota	6	6	6	6

Ohio	6	15	15	6
Oklahoma	3	5	5	3
Oregon	6	6	6	6
Pennsylvania	4	4	4	4
Rhode Island	15	15	10	10
South Carolina	3	3	3	3
South Dakota	3	6	6	6
Tennessee	6	6	6	6
Texas	4	4	4	4
Utah	4	6	6	4
Vermont	6	6	5	3
Virginia	3	5	6	3
Washington	3	6	6	3
West Virginia	5	10	6	5
Wisconsin	6	6	10	6
Wyoming	8	10	10	8

Statute of Limitations That Are Revived or Extended Only By Writing a New Promise to Pay:

(Debtor sending a payment does not revive or extend statute of limitations.)

State Code Section

Arizona	12-508
California	CCP 360
Colorado	13-80-113
Florida	95.4
Iowa	614.11
Kansas	60-250
Maine	14-860

Massachusetts	260-13
Michigan	27A.5866
Minnesota	541.17
Mississippi	15-1-73
Missouri	516.320
Nevada	11.390
New York	GOL 17-101
Texas	16.065
West Virginia	55-2-8
Wisconsin	893.45

Debt Settlement

Now that you understand some of the basics of fixing bad credit, let's talk about debt settlement and credit repair in detail.

Debt settlement can be both on a personal and business side. But look at this: you can settle your debts anywhere from a 40% to 80% discount. One of the things that we teach folks (and I think you might like this) is that a lot of times, what we're finding out when we're dealing with creditors, is that creditors often pay you for the right to settle your debt for zero, because of the way the law is written to protect the consumer, and because of how they do business.

Now, did you catch that? Let me repeat it again: creditors often pay you for the right to settle your debt for zero.

Let's say you've got a $10,000 credit card bill that's overdue. Instead of $10,000, they might say, "Hey, if you'll settle our Citibank credit card for zero, we'll give you $2,000." These are some of the things that we teach folks how to do. It doesn't always happen that way, but sometimes it does.

The laws that give us this ability are:

1. The Fair Credit Reporting Act
2. Fair Debt Collections Practices Act

How to Get Creditors to Pay You $1,000 or More for the Right to Settle Debt for $0

That's a pretty bold statement, wouldn't you say? Imagine turning the tables on some of these unscrupulous creditors to the point where they pay you thousands, settle your account for zero, and ask your forgiveness. You see, no one teaches what I am about to teach you. This is powerful, proven and simple.

So what's the secret? It has to do with how creditors collect the debts that they are owed. In my many years in this business, I have never found a creditor who did not violate the law when it comes to collecting debts. What collectors rely on is the lack of knowledge by the consumer. They know that 98% to 99% of consumers do not know their rights, and they intimidate a consumer into paying debts that they may not even owe. Under the Fair Credit Reporting Act (FCRA) and the Fair Debt Collections Practices Act (FDCPA), the creditor must follow certain rules. If they do not, they are subject to fines for each time they violate the rules.

A Real Life Example

Let me give you a quick example. We had a client that owed $10,000 on a credit card debt and they wanted our help in settling. We determined that the creditor called our client three times in a single day, as well as shared information about our client's debt with some of her co-workers. These are violations. The creditor can only call you once a day, and cannot share information about your debt with anyone else. The creditor had three violations, but here's the kicker. They did the same thing for five days straight, trying to intimidate and embarrass our client. Three violations per day times five days came to 15 violations.

The best news is that usually each violation is a $1,000 fine, so it's money in your pocket. In this case, we allowed the creditor to pay our client $3,000 and to mark the debt as paid in full. Did you get what just happened? We knew the law. The creditor violated the law and ended up paying *us* for the right to settle the debt for zero. If everyone took action when their rights were violated, the credit bureaus would lose a fortune in legal disputes. It's time to protect your rights as a consumer, as well as protecting the rights of your fellow United States citizens.

Take a look at some of the most common violations below:

Who	Why	Precedent/Law	Fine
Creditors, if they report your credit history inaccurately	Defamation, financial injury	US Court of Appeals, Ninth Circuit, No. 00-15946, Nelson vs. Chase Manhattan	Extent of damages incurred by the wronged party as deemed by the courts
Creditors, if you dispute a debt, and they fail to report it as disputed to the credit bureaus	Protection under the FCRA	FCRA Section 623.	$1,000
Creditors, if they pull your credit file without permissible purpose	Injury to your credit report and credit score	FCRA Section 604 (A)(3)	$1,000
Credit bureaus, if they refuse to correct information after being provided proof	Defamation, willful injury	FCRA Section 623 CUSHMAN, v. TRANS UNION CORPORATION US Court of	Extent of damages incurred by the wronged party, as deemed by the courts

		Appeals for the Third Circuit Court Case 115 F.3d 220 June 9, 1997, Filed (D.C. No. 95-cv-01743).	
Credit bureaus, if they reinsert a removed item from your credit report without notifying you in writing within five business days.	Consumer protection afforded by the FCRA	FCRA Part (A)(5)(B)(ii)	$1,000
Credit bureaus, if they fail to respond to your written disputes within 30 days (a 15 day extension may be granted if they receive information from the creditor within the first 30 days)	Consumer protection afforded by the FCRA	FCRA Section 611 Part (A)(1)	$1,000

Collection Agencies, if it is listed as both the purchaser and the "assignee"; it has to be one or the other	Protection under the FDCPA	Gearing v. Check Brokerage Corp 233 F.3d 469 (7th Cir. 2000)	$1000
Collection Agencies, if they mis-represent themselves or the debt, regardless of intent	Protection under the FDCPA	Gearing v. Check Brokerage Corp Cacace v. Lucas, 775 F. Supp. 502, 505 (D. Conn. 1990)	$1000
Creditors or collection agencies, and credit bureaus, if they try and "Re-age" your account by up-dating the date of last activity on your credit report in the hopes of keeping nega-tive informa-tion on your account longer	Consumer protection afforded by the FCRA	FCRA Section 605 (c) Running of the reporting period	$1,000

Collection Agencies, if you dispute a debt and the collection agency fails to report it as disputed to the credit bureaus	Protection under the FDCPA	FDCPA Section 807(8)	$1,000
Collection agencies, if they do not validate your debt, yet continue to pursue collection activity (file for judgments, call or write you)	Consumer protection afforded by the FDCPA	FDCPA Section 809 (b), FTC opinion letter *Cass from LeFevre*	$1,000
Collection agencies, if you have sent them a cease and desist letter and they still call you	Consumer protection afforded by the FDCPA	FDCPA Section 805 (c)	$1,000

Collection agencies, if they have not validated your debt and they still continue to report to the credit bureaus	Consumer protection afforded by the FDCPA	FDCPA Section 809 (b), FTC opinion letter *Cass from LeFevre*	$1,000
Collection agencies, if they: - Cash a post-dated check before the date on the check - Cost you money by making you accept collect calls or COD mail - Take or threaten to take any personal property without a judgment	Consumer protection afforded by the FDCPA	FDCPA 808 Section	$1,000
Collector, if the collector calls you after 9 PM at night or before 8 AM	Consumer protection afforded by the FDCPA	FDCPA Section 805. (a)(1)	$1,000

Collector, if the collector calls you at your place of employment and knows, or has reason to know, that your employer prohibits the consumer from receiving such communication	Consumer protection afforded by the FDCPA	FDCPA Section 805. (a)(3)	$1,000
Collection Agencies, if they call any third party about your debt, such as friends, neighbors, relatives, etc. However they can contact your attorney, a consumer reporting agency, the creditor, the attorney of the creditor, or the attorney of the debt collector.	Consumer protection afforded by the FDCPA	FDCPA Section 805. (b)	$1,000

Collection agency, if it uses any kind of harassment or abuse**	Consumer protection afforded by the FDCPA	FDCPA Section 806	$1,000
Collector, if the collector claims to garnish your wages, seize property or have you arrested ***	Consumer protection afforded by the FDCPA	FDCPA Section 807	$1,000
Collection agencies, if they did not sue you in the county in which you lived when you signed the original contract for the debt, or where you live at the time when they file the lawsuit	Consumer protection afforded by the FDCPA	FDCPA Section 811 (a) (2)	$1,000 Also a good grounds for getting a judgment vacated

** (1) The use or threat of use of violence or other criminal means to harm the physical person, reputation, or property of any person. (2) The use of obscene or profane language or language the natural consequence of which is to abuse the hearer or reader. (3) The publication of a list of consumers who allegedly refuse to pay debts, except to a consumer reporting agency. (4) The advertisement for sale of any debt to coerce payment of the debt. (5) Causing a telephone to ring or engaging any person in telephone conversation repeatedly or continuously with intent to annoy, abuse, or harass any person at the called number. (6) Placement of telephone calls without meaningful disclosure of the caller's identity.

The FCRA gives several different federal agencies authority to enforce the FCRA:

FOR QUESTIONS OR CONCERNS REGARDING	PLEASE CONTACT
CRAs, creditors and others not listed below	Federal Trade Commission Consumer Response Center- FCRA Washington, DC 20580 * 202-326-3761
National banks, federal branches/agencies of foreign banks (word "National" or initials "N.A." appear in or after bank's name)	Office of the Comptroller of the Currency Compliance Management, Mail Stop 6-6 Washington, DC 20219 * 800-613-6743
Federal Reserve System member banks (except national banks, and federal branches/ agencies of foreign banks)	Federal Reserve Board Division of Consumer & Community Affairs Washington, DC 20551 * 202-452-3693
Savings associations and federally chartered savings banks (word "Federal" or initials "F.S.B." appear in federal institution's name)	Office of Thrift Supervision Consumer Programs Washington D.C. 20552* 800- 842-6929

Federal credit unions (words "Federal Credit Union" appear in institution's name)	National Credit Union Administration 1775 Duke Street Alexandria, VA 22314 * 703-518-6360
State-chartered banks that are not members of the Federal Reserve System	Federal Deposit Insurance Corporation Division of Compliance & Consumer Affairs Washington, DC 20429 * 800-934-FDIC
Air, surface, or rail common carriers regulated by former Civil Aeronautics Board or Interstate Commerce Commission	Department of Transportation Office of Financial Management Washington, DC 20590 * 202-366-1306
Activities subject to the Packers and Stockyards Act, 1921	Department of Agriculture Office of Deputy Administrator-GIPSA Washington, DC 20250 * 202-720-7051

Conclusion

So, in a nutshell, debt settlement is pretty easy. You just need to know your rights. Once you do, you are in the driver's seat. Settling your debts at a 40% to 80% discount happens all the time; it's easy. We can guarantee that all day long.

Here are some things to consider:

1. **Most unsecured debts can be settled.** An unsecured debt is a debt where there is no collateral. Unsecured debts include medical bills, credit cards, department store cards, personal loans, collection accounts, student loans, amounts remaining after foreclosure or repossession, and bounced checks. There are a few creditors who will never compromise, but most will take a less-than-full payment as settlement-in-full to close a

troublesome account. (Utility companies, however, rarely settle for less than the full balance.)

2. **Secured, collateralized debts (such as a home or automobile loans)** are an entirely different story. If the creditor can simply repossess the property, why negotiate? You can often renegotiate a short payment relief with a secured debt, but don't attempt to settle the account while you still possess the property.

Also, the creditor must have a good reason to want to settle. If the account is paid current and there is no recent history of late payment, there is no reason for the creditor to believe that they are in danger of not getting paid. Just place yourself in the creditor's shoes. If you were getting your monthly payments on time, would you settle for a discount?

> I am in no way advocating that you stop paying your bills. I am simply stating what the creditors' expectations are, and their response to your offers based on the circumstances. This is not legal or accounting advice. If you need legal or accounting advice, please refer to a competent licensed professional.

CHAPTER 8

SECRET PLACES TO FIND MONEY

So far, I've gone into depth about what business credit is, why you need it, and the eight steps that will ensure you can get it. Now it's time to talk about some of the other resources and strategies that can bring massive infusions of money into your business – many of which are 100% risk free.

Who Knew?

A lot of people don't know that Costco and Sam's Club have credit cards, which each have up to a $100,000 line of credit. They are two of my favorite places, simply because once you have a history with them, and once you have a business credit score, you can apply for that $100,000.

Sam's Club has two lines of credit; a private line of credit and a Discover card line of credit. I tell people to stay away from the Discover card at first. However, if you have an existing personal account with either, you can transfer it over to your business account. Stay with the private label, which means that your line of credit only applies to purchases made at Sam's. This is why: if you have a personal account, switching to a business account will give you a head start; it will transfer your previous account activity.

If you start a new business account, I recommend that you buy business supplies, groceries, whatever you want under your business account, and show at least three months of buying activity, and three months of timely payments. Then, they will then offer you a larger line of credit that you can go after. You don't want to just apply when you have no affiliation with them.

Friends and Family

If you have a great business idea that you've always wanted to start, the best place to get funding is to start with the people who believe in you: your friends and family. Go to that trusted friend and ask him or her to invest in you. Remember, the loans from friends do not appear on your credit report. Just make sure that if you borrow from your friends that you outline everything on paper, which serves as a contract. This solves any issues of how the money is to be paid back and helps to keep the friendship intact. The other thing is to always pay according to the terms of your agreement. If you need to get the business started before you start making payments, write it out in your contract.

Leverage Your Assets

You can also borrow money against something that you own. For instance, a car, stereo, TV – whatever you can think of. You can use your personal property as collateral for the loan. Keep in mind that if you take out a loan like this and don't pay it back, you could lose your property, and you will pay a very high interest rate.

HELOC (Home Equity Line of Credit)

If you own a home, you can use the home as collateral by getting what's called a home equity line of credit. This allows you to borrow against your home. This can give you a large sum of cash that you can use to start or expand your business.

Most banks allow you to borrow against the equity in your home. Equity is the difference between what the property is worth on the current market and what you owe. If you have other mortgages on the home, you need to subtract those from the value of the property too. If you own the home free and clear, then you have 100% equity and you can borrow against the entire value of the property.

Barter Financing

Barter financing is nothing more than trading something you have with someone else that has something you need. Typically, you trade at full market value. For example, the owner of a printing company may

114

need a new website designed, so he trades with a marketing company who needs new marketing materials printed. They are able to trade their services and both of them get what they need.

Contract Financing

Contract financing involves having your clients prepay for your services or materials. If you charge for monthly maintenance plans or have servicing programs, you can charge your clients before the services are performed, rather than after they are completed. If you are just starting out, you could offer new clients a discount for an annual contract and use the upfront cash to jump-start your business.

Timeshare

Timesharing refers to taking some of your unused or under-utilized equipment and renting it out to people who don't have the ability to buy the equipment on their own. In fact, you can rent it out to multiple people at the same time who just use it as they need it. You can charge them up front on a monthly basis, or even give them a discount for paying for an annual lease. Here's another idea: allow your new timeshare partners to use your facility or equipment at night when you are not using it. This allows the equipment to be used 24 hours a day.

Renting

One of the mistakes I see many new business owners make is that they go out and buy lots of equipment and use up all the cash that they have. Instead, take a look at renting the equipment. Renting allows you to conserve your cash and just make small monthly payments. Now you can conserve your cash for marketing or anything else you need. Almost everything your business needs can be rented. When you rent, try to look for a rental agreement that allows the payments to be applied towards the purchase of the equipment. This way you will own the equipment after a set period of time.

Buy an Existing Business with Its Own Money

One of the things I teach some of my clients who are looking for cash to start a business is to consider the possibility of buying an operating business instead of starting from scratch. Did you know that you can buy a business using the business' own cash? Sounds cool, right? Let me give you a few ideas of how you could make this happen. The important thing I want you to get from this Guerrilla source of cash is that you can buy the business, even if the seller wants cash, without using any of your own money.

Did you catch that?

I said *none of your own cash*. You can use the cash that already exists in the business as your down payment. This includes any cash that is already in the business' bank accounts. You can also use accounts receivable. What I mean by this is that you can borrow against the money that is owed to the business. This technique is called factoring.

It's important for me to restate that it's not your money. I'm just describing how you get some of the money. So one of the things that you can do is use assets of the very business that you're buying to pay for its actual purchase. And, yes, it's true; you can do that. And get this: yes, you can count on the seller of the business for the money that you need to actually buy a business. This is one of the ways that we can buy a business with its own cash.

I like using OPM – or Other People's Money. In fact, I love using OPM to buy a business. It allows me to leverage the business better. I have none of my cash at risk and I can increase my profit. I always like to have extra cash sitting around. And let's assume that you're interested in buying a business and you have no cash; then this would be a perfect option for you.

To prove it to you, let me give you a few examples of people who chose the path of buying a business versus starting from scratch. In fact, I could give you story after story after story, but let me tell you about some companies that you may have heard of. By the time we get to the end of the story, you'll realize, "Gosh, I know that brand." And you'll see that they all started their companies with none of their own cash. They were able to bootstrap it, meaning they were able to do it without financial help from others.

Let me give you the first. This is from a guy named Ray Kroc. Now, Ray Kroc was a 52-year-old milkshake salesman back in 1955 when he convinced brothers Mac and Dick McDonald to sell him a lonely little hamburger stand, which was located near Burbank, California. Now, Kroc didn't have any money to speak of, so he worked out a really unique and highly leveraged no-cash-down lease arrangement. On its first day in business, Kroc's cash register rang up $366.12. "It rained that day," he later explained. The following week, his daily sales doubled. Today, the registers at McDonald's ring up a bit more than that, taking in upwards of $20 billion a year.

McDonald's is both the biggest owner of commercial real estate and the biggest food service corporation in America. And Ray Kroc didn't have to spend a penny of his own to get started. The fact that McDonald's is one of the largest owners of real estate may come as a surprise to some, but think about it: they own the best locations in every single city. They're on all the corners because those properties are worth more. McDonald's is about systems and real estate. It's not about burgers.

Here's another example about a gentleman named Paul Orfalea. He was known as a C-student, just out of college when he started the now-famous Kinkos copy stores without a penny of his own money. It began in 1971, when he convinced a commercial bank that there was a demand among college students for a convenient, multi-purpose coffee shop. The bank loaned him $5,000 to take over an 80-square-foot hamburger stand for that purpose. And Orfalea went on to build his tiny operation into a $400 million chain of nearly 800 stores throughout America.

Then there's the famous confectioner William Wrigley Jr. in 1891, carmaker Henry Ford in 1903, Reader's Digest publishers DeWitt and Lila Wallace in 1922 – all bootstrapped entrepreneurs using other people's money to lay down a foundation for great business fortunes.

So think about it. These were some people who went out and either started and leveraged a business, got a bank loan, got a lease, were able to use the business assets to fund the business, or to get terms with creditors. But they were all able to bootstrap their startup so that it required none of their own cash to get into the business. These are some ideas that I talk about in my other book called *How to Buy a Business Using Its Own Cash*. Would you like a copy? If so just go to our website and you can download a copy for free.

Purchase Order Financing

Purchase order financing is also called work-in-process financing, or financing that is based on your company's invoices, purchase orders, or back orders. Money gets released based on each order as it comes in.

Private Flooring of Inventory

Flooring is a term used by banks that lend money for the purchase of durable goods like cars, TVs, windows, plumbing supplies, etc. The bank will own the inventory until it's sold off the floor. Instead of going to a bank for financing, you can approach private investors to give you the same financing and use the durable goods as collateral. An example of this is Rachel, who ran an appliance outlet store. She got private investors to put up the cash to buy the appliances that she sold at her store. With each sale, she'd first pay the investor back at a great rate of return. This allowed the investor to be profitable, and allowed Rachel a fast way to purchase inventory so that she could jumpstart her business without going to the bank or worrying about credit checks.

Bank Deposits or CD's

If you already have money in CD's, you may be able to borrow against the CD at a very favorable rate. If you have stocks and bonds, you can typically borrow 50% of its value – sometimes more. You can also borrow against some life insurance policies if you have one.

Get a Co-signer

Sometimes the easiest solution is right in front of you. Ask a friend, relative or business associate to co-sign on a loan with you. You can combine both your credit and his or her credit to get a loan. If your co-signor has good credit and yours is bad, you can still get a loan by using the other person's strong credit. This is perfectly legal.

Royalties

Have you ever watched the show *Shark Tank*? The premise of the show is for new inventors to approach private investors on the show (the sharks) with their ideas and see if the sharks would be interested in buying into their business and help them make it grow. Every once in a while, an investor comes up with a unique idea that would be better off being licensed to a large company like Wal-Mart that already has the distribution channels in place. In essence, the inventor licenses the right to their product to another company that will sell it through a company like Wal-Mart. The inventor does not get a huge amount of money upfront; rather, he or she gets a percentage of every item that is sold. Sometimes the investor can get a lump sum of cash up front, plus a monthly royalty.

This is great for the inventor because it gets the product out into the marketplace, where it generates a steady stream of income without the hassles of development, marketing, distribution, sales or customer service. A smaller piece of a much bigger pie is often better than trying to do everything on your own. Royalties or licensing fees can pay for a lot of inventions, or to help you grow your business in new directions.

Your Own Company's Capital

You can use your own company's capital in creative ways to pay for the things you need. Here are a few ideas:

- Offer discounts for early payment of invoices.
- Force slow-paying customers to pay in advance with cash on their next order.
- Reduce terms for payments from 60 days to 30 or 15 days.
- Pay your bills on the last possible date, or even ask your suppliers for more lenient terms.
- Increase your prices slightly. This is known as a nuisance increase. It's not high enough to make the customer leave, but it will generate extra revenue for you.
- Open mail as soon as it arrives and deposit any checks you receive the same day.
- Sell off unused equipment or inventory.

Unclaimed Funds

I learned this technique from a good friend of mine who finds money that is owed to people. He does this for a fee, but you don't need to hire him; you can do all of this on your own for free. In fact, this technique was covered on an Oprah show once, and was very popular. Oprah had experts show that nine out of 10 people are owed some money. The various websites show that there is an estimated $400 billion in unclaimed money that is owed to people around the country. How much are you owed?

According to these websites, the state of New York has unclaimed bank accounts and security deposits that total over $5 billion. California has over $3 billion. And get this: the United States Treasury has $1.3 billion in unredeemed savings bonds that have never been cashed in. One of those big credit card companies that issues travelers checks for people when they travel has over $3.8 billion in traveler checks that have been issued and never cashed! Even the IRS is in on the game. The IRS estimates that tax refunds totaling over $25 billion have never been cashed. Wow!

There could be a lot of money out there in your name. Even people who lost their home to foreclosure could be owed thousands of dollars in what's called an overage. Even it is nothing more than some rebates you are owed from a department store for $100 or $200, it all adds up. That money can be used to start your business or pay off some of your other debts. The states and counties don't tell you this because if you don't claim the money after a certain period of time, then the state or county gets to keep all those billions.

Free Money

Do you love free money? I do, and I think you do, too. Most people think that to get money you have to work hard or there must be some hidden catch that you don't see. Well, I am about to show you how easy it is to get money that you never have to pay back.

This is huge; think about it for a moment. Imagine getting $5,000, $10,000, even $30,000 in free money that you can use to start or grow your business and you never have to pay it back. It's money that does not appear on your personal credit report or your business credit report.

Why do you work for money? No, really; why do you work for money? If you really think about it, you don't work for money to pay your bills (which I know is part of it) so much as you work so that you can have the lifestyle you want – to do the things you want, with the people you want, in the timeframe that you want. Ultimately, we are working for more time. When you don't have to work to get money and it is just handed to you, then that means you have more "free" time to do those things that are important to you.

Free Money from the Government

Did you know that the government wants to give you money to start your business? They just want to give it to you and say, "Here's the money." Thousands, hundreds of thousands, even millions of dollars that you can use for your business – for any little pet project that you can possibly think of – the money is there waiting for you to just take it. Unfortunately, most people don't know that the money is there. The government is willing to give you money right now, today, for the basics you need in order to start your business. Because you have a corporation, you have access to that.

Let's talk about where to begin. First off, I want to say that the government has billions of dollars in grants that most people don't even know exist. The government doesn't advertise this. They don't take out TV ads or radio spots, they don't advertise in newspaper or on billboards. They don't even tell you about it when you fill out your taxes. They don't do any of that. As a big business (and of course that's where you're headed), you need to know all about this kind of money; you need to know the secret.

It's All Yours

The nice thing that I love about grants is that they are not loans. Grant money comes from your tax dollars, so grant money is your money. It's money the government takes in, moves around a bit, and gives back out – to folks just like you and me. But think about it: all that grant money, all those billions and trillions of dollars, is your money, your kids' money, your grandkids' money. They are not loans. A grant is money that is given to you – money that you do not ever have to repay.

Now, it's true you could go to the Small Business Administration and take out a small business loan at a low interest rate with very reasonable terms for repayment. You could do that, but if the government is willing to give you money for free that you don't ever have to pay back, wouldn't that be a better way to start your business? Imagine what your business and your life would be like.

Say you applied for, and got, a grant for $100,000 to start your business. What would you do with the money? Would you spend it on advertising? Would you spend it on office equipment or supplies? There are all sorts of things you could use it for to grow your business, right? Hiring staff, doing research – doing the things that you want to do. There are no limits to what you can do with grant money when it comes to your projects.

Real Life Examples

Let me give some real life examples: $75,000 a year salary – free money; $6,000 a year in healthcare for an entire family of six – free money; $6,000 a year into a 401(k), IRA – free money; $120,000 a year expense account – free money; $10,000 a month – free money; $6,000 a year car payment at $500 a month – free money; $12,000 a year for your business, for your laptop, supplies, Internet – free money; $48,000 a year for your office lease – free money; $4,000 a month paid toward a 5,000 square-feet commercial building – free money. And the list of these real-life examples could go on and on.

Grant money allows you to continue on as an entrepreneur while you build systems. You hire the project staff to implement the project, and you keep moving forward to $25,000 a year for "program assistant" – free money. In total, you have $298,000 a year in free money just for you to carry the project forward.

The government is essentially giving you the money to go out and start your business so that you then create jobs, pay taxes and reinvest money back into the economy. That's why they give you the money.

Now, this money can go to anyone who asks for it – including you. Sometimes there are limitations on some of the government programs, but not for all of them. There have been a number of millionaires and even very, very large corporations – names that would shock you if we listed them here – that have taken advantage of all of these programs. You can and you should do the same thing. There are hundreds of thousands of these different programs out there. Some have very small restrictions on how you spend the money, some have none.

It is Easier Than You Think

Getting the money is usually a matter of just making a couple of phone calls or filling out a basic application. That's usually all it takes, although some do require lots of paperwork; it depends on the type of the grant. You can find grants that merely require an easy-to-complete form of information that you already know – easy peasy, as I like to call it.

Here's a question that I hear a lot: "How many offices are there out there that give grants, or is there only one main area that you go to?" The answer is that there are tons of offices that work on grants. The government is a huge network. You can't find one that just says "free money." It doesn't work like that. You need to know where to go, where to look, and how to do it.

Sometimes it takes a little bit of research to find the right program that meets your specific needs, but a small amount of your time spent doing the research can mean receiving that free money that never needs to be paid back. Not a bad trade, wouldn't you agree?

We Can Help

We also associate with a couple of different companies that will actually find these grants for you. So, if you're interested in having somebody else do the research for you to find the grants, to find them specific for your business, your industry, your company, and to actually do all the paperwork for you and get you the grant, guess what? Just visit our website for an updated list of companies that can help you with all your grant writing needs. They do charge a small fee (so full disclosure there), but they will do all of the work for you.

It's Really Free

Let me just restate some of the things that we already talked about. Government grants are available to not only large corporations, but to small corporations like yours – to individuals, to nonprofits, they're available to everyone; they're not just in the good ol' boy system, and they're not just for the companies who know all the rules. They're available for everyone who wants to reach out and take the money. It's up to you. You have to reach out. True, you have to put forth a little bit of effort, but when you think about what you can do with all of that free money – thousands, even hundreds of thousands of dollars – don't you think it's worth doing a little bit of research?

Keep in mind that these grants can be used to just pay your current bills, whatever they are – for your children's education, to start your own business, to pay property taxes, to put food on the table, to buy clothes, whatever you can think of.

The Hardest Part

Some people are not even aware that all this free money exists. Others know that there is free money out there, and they may even try to find it, but they quickly get overwhelmed by the amount of research that needs to be done. They just don't know where to go or what the online right search terms are that would lead to some of this free money.

Having the Internet now has made this job so much easier and so much faster. The Internet can be your best friend when looking for grant money. Even if you don't have a home computer, you can use one for free at your local library or go to a friend's house. Simply having access and knowing that this information is available is half the battle.

Let's talk about some of the websites that I like. Here's one website, www.govbenefits.gov. Now, this site has information on thousands of programs. It's very easy to use and navigate, which I really like because I don't like complicated stuff. Some websites can seem confusing and downright intimidating, and I like it when they make it really easy for us.

Start Here

If you go to the site, one of the things that you should look for is a big "start now" button. I like that because if you're just starting your search, you may not know where to go, what you're looking for, or even what category you should be searching in yet. You just know that you want some free money, but you're not sure where to start. So just click on the "start now" button, and it'll take you to an easy-to–answer, basic questionnaire. It will take you about five to 10 minutes to go through the entire questionnaire, and the questions themselves are simple and pretty straightforward. You're not giving out any private information; it just helps point you in the right direction.

After you've answered the questions, it will list some possible grants or benefit programs that you might be eligible for. That's it. It's very, very simple.

If you already know what you want the grant for, use the quick-search feature and type in what you're looking for, like "nail care," "yard care business," or "Chinese restaurant" – whatever it is you want the grant for. You would be amazed at the different industries these smaller Mom and Pop businesses have gotten grant money for in order to start and to keep themselves in operation, keep the entire family's food on the table, and to employ everybody.

Once you're on the site and you're looking at things, I would encourage you to just click on different things that interest you and start reading. Learn about the different programs available, what they look for, and the amount of monies that are available. In fact, you may see an area that will give you an idea for starting a business that you hadn't thought of before, and you may want to shift the focus of your current business – or at least create another division that would fall into a different area – just so that you can get some of the applicable grant money.

Another great website for finding grant information is a website called www.grants.gov. This site is great because a lot of federal agencies actually post their grants right there. You can find out about the grant, read about it, and see if you qualify. You can even download applications so you can fill it out and do everything online.

Instead of having to search through hundreds of different programs, this site allows you to see what you might apply for and what you might qualify for, and you get to do it all in one location. Currently, there are in excess of 1,000 different grant programs from almost 30 agencies on the site, equating to a total of about $400 billion in grant awards.

Another thing that's really nice about the www.grants.gov site is that you only have to enter your information one time and you get to search through all the different grants through almost 30 different agencies. You can do research on grant money by category or by agency name. There's tons of money available – billions and billions. All you have to do is do the research and you get your piece of the pie.

Isn't America beautiful?

If you're not sure what you're looking for, and you just want to browse around without revealing who you are or anything about yourself or your business, you can absolutely do it on this site. That's one of the features I like. Until you know what you want to do, just browse around and see what's there, and then just register when you find something you like.

There are some basic instructions on the website. They also have a really good user guide that is available at www.grants.gov/assets/ApplicantUserGuide.pdf..

One thing to always keep in mind is that you can also go to the Small Business Administration, or www.SBA.gov, which has all sorts of loans and low interest rate loans that are great for starting a business and getting some of the capital that you need.

There are even private foundations that lend money. Here are a couple of sites: www.foundationcenter.org/getstarted/individuals/ and www.fundsnetservices.com. They literally have hundreds of different sites that you can go to. There are hundreds of different programs, and there's billions and billions of dollars' worth of money that's available for you to start your business for any purpose that you can possibly think of.

Here is a quick list that will be invaluable to you:

Federal Money Programs

- www.Grants.gov
- www.ed.gov/about/offices/list/ocfo/grants/grants.html
- www.grantsolutions.gov
- www.grants.gov/assets/GDG_AppUserGuide_0207.pdf
- www.sba.gov – Small Business Administration
- www.fsa.usda.gov – $200K to run a ranch or farm.
- www.dla.cmil.db – $300K to help get government contracts.
- www.rurdev.usda.gov – up to $10 million to start a business in a small town.
- www.sba.gov/INV/venture.html – up to $3 million in venture capital.

Private Sources for Free Money and Grants

- www.foundationcenter.com/getstarted/individuals/
- www.Fundsnetservices.com
- www.womensnet.net
- www.ehome-basedbusiness.com/articles/
- www.dressforsuccess.org – free clothes
- www.bottomlesscloset.org – free clothes
- www.fns.usda.gov/cnd/lunch or
  www.fns.usda.gov/fdd/programs/nsip
  - www.idanetwork.org
  - www.adea.org
  - www.aoa.org
  - www.helpingpatients.org
  - www.hud.gov/offices/
  - www.hud.gov/office/cpd/affordablehousing/programs/home/addi/
  - www.ftc.gov
  - www.ed.gov/about/offices/list/fsa/index.html
  - www.ed.gov/about/offices/list/ope/iegps/index.html
  - www.ed.gov/programs/iegpsirs/index.html
  - www.studentaid.ed.gov
  - www.rankinfoundation.org

- www.aauw.org/fga/fellowships_grants/
- www.grants.nih.gov/grants/index.cfm
- www.ed.gov/about/offices/list/ocfo/grants/grants
- www.spencer.org/programs/grants/research_grants.htm
- www.energystar.gov
- www.hud.gov/economicdevelopment/index.cfm
- www.taxcreditcompany.com
- www.ntctac.com
- www.firstgov.gov
- www.pueblo.gsa.gov/call
- www.rurdev.usda.gov
- www.staff.lib.msu.edu/harris23/grants/3women.htm – A compilation of funding opportunities for women.

Information at Your Fingertips

There is tons of information out there that's free, so you don't need to buy any e-books or programs that teach you how to find grants. The programs on how to find this money are right there, available at your fingertips. Most people don't realize they can access this information for free, which is why they end up buying costly, inaccurate reports over the Internet. But because you have this book, you have the inside track. Now you know where to go look, which makes your job so much easier.

Let me elaborate just a little bit more. The main United States website for the federal government is www.usa.gov and it has information on all the different government agencies, including, at the very top of the website, a list for benefits and grants. This link gives you a ton of official information on grants, loans, financial aid, student loans, benefits, all from the United States government. You can be set up an e-mail notification list so that if anything changes, you'll automatically receive the update. I absolutely love it.

Here's a site for another little gem that I love. It's called www.govloans.gov; this is a website for government loan programs. This site will direct you to all the different loan information that helps meet your needs. This is an outstanding source for finding loans for your business, disaster relief, education, college, housing, or for the support of veterans and children. At this site, you can pretty much get information on anything you can think of that you might need a loan for.

According to the United States government, over a million people a year are getting free money and cheap loans from the government. What's great about grants, again, is you never have to pay the money back. Once the government gives it to you, it's yours. You can use it for its intended purposes, and you never have to pay it back; there's no interest, no payments, no nothing. It's wonderful.

I have another exciting program to tell you about. The SBA Office of Technology has what's called the Small Business Technology Transfer program, or STTR. There are five federal departments that award a combined $2 billion to small businesses and small high-tech businesses in this program. If you have a small business in this type of industry and you have less than five employees, guess what? You can apply for and get a piece of that $2 billion chunk of money that's available.

Think about this right now. The Department of Energy, the Department of Health and Human Services, the Department of Defense, the National Science Foundation and NASA have a percentage of their R&D budget allocated for this program. The SBA actually coordinates between those that apply for the grants and those agencies. The dollars are big, the work is hugely important, and the money could be yours by applying today. This is very, very good stuff.

There is federal grant or federal money programs for just about everything that you could think of. For instance, you could get $300,000 to help you get a government contract at www.dla.mil/db. There's a $200,000 credit line for a small business at www.sba.gov/financing/loanprog/caplines.tml.

There's a $25,000 microloan and $500,000 to start a business available at www.sba.gov. At www.fsa.usda.gov, you can get information on a $200,000 grant for running a ranch or a farm. There's $500,000 in government contracts for females and minorities at www.osdbuweb.gov. There's even $3 million in venture capital available at www.sba.gov/INV/venture.html.

This is incredible. All you have to do is start doing research. You can get free money. You don't even have to think about getting lines of credit when you're dipping into all the free money that's available to you right now. So you have lots of free money, government grants, and low interest loans available to start your business, help give it a jumpstart, expand it, or to start a whole new business altogether.

There's also another program that's put out by the Small Business Investment Company, or SBIC. This entity, started in 1958, provides venture capital to small businesses that really want to grow. This program has been around for over 50 years, but few people get onto the list because they don't know about it. That's kind of sad in my book; all this free money that's available to help you start your business and you don't even know that it's there to help you.

What's nice about this program is that it doesn't focus on a single business. In fact, it could be any type of business, any industry, any area of the country.

Let's say that you want to get some expert coaching or management advice that will help take you to the next level. The SBIC can actually help you do this. If you go to www.sba.gov/aboutsba/ sbaprograms/inv/index.html, the SBIC actually has funding for small businesses, with as much as $10 billion from the government and another $12 billion from private funding sources to help you. The SBIC website states, "The most exciting potential of an SBIC investment is how it can turn one small company into a great success story."

Imagine for a moment that you're in the ranks of some of these big names who were once small companies – companies like America Online, Staples, Federal Express, Jenny Craig, Apple Computer, Gymboree; names I'm sure you've heard of. All of these companies have used these types of loans and programs. You won't be the first to claim the free money that's available to you. It *can* be yours.

Now, if you are a woman reading this book, or you have a female business partner, you're in luck. There are some additional programs just for women. The Small Business Association's Office of Women's Business Ownership is designed to help improve their communities by providing women assistance with starting a business. The association will help the business by getting the owners trained on how to get started and how to maintain a successful business; there's lots of help. You can check it out at www.sba.gov/aboutsba/sba programs/onlinewbc/index.html.

Let's say that you're a teacher at a private school or public school, or you're a principal and you need money for your school and its different programs. The website www.schoolgrants.org, which has a tagline called, "The one-stop site for pre-K-12 school grant opportunities," is perfect for you. The site offers grant-writing tips and workshops on how to write successful grants in the area of education. In addition, it provides a list of grants where you can find information and opportunities. So if you want to work in the educational field, this is the site you want to go to.

So those are some great sites to get you started. The world is your oyster. All you have to do is open it up and claim that pearl.

CHAPTER 9

SYSTEMATIZE YOUR BUSINESS

Now that we have thoroughly discussed ways to pump your business full of resources, it's time to talk about strategies to help you maximize those resources. As you secure those massive lines of credit and other financial resources, you can make them go even further by thoroughly systemizing your business. This will not only help you to magnify the power of each dollar, but will enable you to work less so you can spend the time you want to on the things you enjoy. After all, isn't that what this whole game is about?

But most people start to get uptight when they hear any talk of systemizing anything, much less a business. Their thoughts immediately turn to the idea of an endless array of meetings that produce a mountain of action items that must be followed up on at the next meeting so even more action items can be generated. In short, people see systemization as some ongoing, convoluted series of processes that only make things more complicated and kill the entrepreneurial spirit.

There is a good chance that you also have this rather bleak view of systemization. Before going any further, let's define what systemization is and what it isn't:

What Systemization Is Not

To be systemized does not mean to be caught up in so many policies and procedures that there is no time left to do anything productive. Systemization is not about filling time or creating the illusion of being busy. A systemized person is not someone who is so hard-nosed that any deviation from the plan is considered scandalous or harmful to the organization.

In short, systemization is not about creating a machine and being dominated by that machine. It does not have to be complicated, function for some unknown reason, or even remain the same from one year to the next.

What Systemization Is

True systemization is more or less the opposite of what most people think it is. In reality, a truly systemized organization has a solid functioning procedure, knows what must be done, has a way to do it, and gets the job done. When a business is truly systemized, there is time to devote to other pastimes. This requires making good use of that creativity that is so common to true entrepreneurs.

With a properly systemized company, the procedures make sense and always have a purpose. There is no room for empty actions that stir up a lot of dust, but accomplish nothing. Within this framework, everyone knows what to do and when to do it. There are no endless meetings to contend with, no complicated policies to observe, and no time wasted spinning the wheels.

That is not to say that every process within a properly systemized company is fun. Few people find the tasks of calculating and paying taxes to be fun, for example. Still, the tasks, if organized properly, can be completed in a reasonable amount of time and leave the rest of the day to move on to something that is more interesting, such as earning new customers, working on a new product, or writing new sales copy.

The bottom line is that true systemization frees you, while a lack of properly systemized organization creates nothing but endless work and stifles you and your business until both are ready to give up – regardless of the size of your credit lines.

Why You Should Systemize Your Business

Now that you understand that systemization is a good thing, let's explore just exactly how this approach to your business is good. There are actually quite a number of benefits that come with creating an organized and systematic environment for your business. Here are some examples:

133

- You can measure your progress. Sure, money coming in is one measure. But what if you could also figure out how to measure how well things are coming with that next big ad campaign, or the development on a new ancillary product that will enhance your main product? If your business is organized, it is possible to do a quick check on these and other ongoing processes and get real-time data on what is going on any time you like.

- Little things get done on time. Without some basic plan for each day, the little things that keep operations going can build up and eventually create a bottleneck. For example, if the posting on the Accounts Receivable and Payable are not being done on a regular schedule, you could find yourself with a lot of work to do when it comes time to cut paychecks to employees or calculate your taxes for the current period. An organized system helps to ensure you don't run into situations where your back is to the wall and you have to drop other tasks in order to play catch-up.

- There is automatically time built in to work on business networking. If your business is systematic in its operations and functions, this means you can spend some time in networking activities that will help your business grow. You'll be able to devote an afternoon to submitting online ads, sending promotional emails, or even promoting your business locally at Chamber of Commerce events. Best of all, you can spend your time on these endeavors knowing that the company is moving right along without your direct attention for a few hours.

- You can take time off. After all, wasn't getting control of your time one of the reasons you wanted to set up your business in the first place? If your business is systematically organized, you can take time off for your son's Little League game, or your daughter's dance recital. There is also the chance that you can even take several days off in order to take a short vacation, if you like. Best of all, you can do this without getting any permission or approval from anyone else, and rest assured your business will continue to move forward in your absence.

At this juncture, it would be a good idea to take a moment and evaluate your own circumstances. Make a list of what it is you want to accomplish with your business. Don't hold back anything, no matter how small, vague, or inconsequential it may seem. If one of the reasons you want your own business is so you can play poker every Thursday night, instead of working a part-time job to make ends meet, put it down. Should your goals have to do with finally being able to afford a two-week vacation every year without worrying about how much money you spend, add it to the list.

Once you have the list written, put it to one side and keep reading. We'll come back and address the list a little later and relate it to the process of systemization in ways you may not have considered up to this point.

A Lesson Learned From the Book "The E-Myth"

Michael Gerber
E-MYTH AUTHOR

Since 1985, there's been one book that has become something like scripture for many entrepreneurs. That book is *The E-Myth*, by Michael E. Gerber. While the book was originally focused on business systemization in the world of brick and mortar companies, subsequent editions have included data that includes an even wider spectrum of businesses, including service-based industries and Internet commerce.

The phrase "e-myth" is short for the Entrepreneurial Myth, which is easily one of the main reasons businesses of any type fail. Basically, this myth holds that if someone is an expert in a particular field, he or she should have no trouble setting up a successful business. After all, they have the vision, right?

Gerber systemically dissects this myth and lays it out for the fallacy it truly is. Within the pages of *The E-Myth*, there are many lessons to learn that can help a fledgling business owner, or even someone who wants to start a business, to avoid a lot of ideas and situations that ultimately lead to failure. However, there is one core lesson that you should take away from Gerber's work, if nothing else in the book sticks with you.

Work On It, Not In It

That one lesson is to not work *in* your business, but to work *on* your business.

But what does that mean? Is Gerber urging business owners to be detached from the business, allowing others to handle everything as he or she blithely goes in whatever direction they wish to go?

Not at all. The point Gerber is making is that the true entrepreneur sets up a system that is able to allow the business to function efficiently, and with the full participation of the business owner. But, the business owner is not bogged down in having to take care of so many different tasks that there is no room left to grow (or work on) the business.

So How Do I Work ON My Business Without Working IN My Business?

One easy way to think of the distinction between these two states is to think of working in your business as essentially having a job. With this job, you have assigned tasks that you do over and over again. Your focus is on those tasks, leaving you little or no time to think of any other tasks or functions that may be going on at the same time you plod through your own assigned list of tasks.

From this perspective, being "in" your business is a lot like working for someone else. When you are an employee, you don't spend much time wondering what tasks the VP of Marketing is doing, or how the Accounting department works. You handle things in your own little world, collect your paycheck, and go your merry way.

By contrast, working "on" your business encompasses a lot more territory. As a business owner, you must think in terms of the entire organization, instead of just one little corner of the business operation. This means you can't afford to be bogged down in tasks associated with one area. If you want to be successful, you must always have a view of the big picture.

Being able to see the big picture and work on growing your business is where the idea of systemization comes in. You create and implement systems that allow all those little things to work while you're focusing on a broader view of things. Working on your business means you don't have to do everything yourself, and you don't have to micro-manage anyone you've hired to do specific tasks for you. If the system is designed properly, the day-to-day aspects of the business will continue with or without your attention, effectively freeing you to spend your days working on making the business stronger, more profitable, and bigger than ever before.

The Lesson to Take Away From "The E-Myth"

In a nutshell, if you don't get anything else from Gerber's book, make sure you get this:

- You don't have to do everything yourself in your business to make it successful.
- You don't have to involve yourself in every last bit of minutiae related to the daily operation of your business.
- You must always keep yourself in a position to see the "big picture" of where your business is going, like we discussed at the very beginning of this book.
- You must allow yourself to steer the ship without worrying if the guys in the hold are feeding the coal into the boiler properly.

One of the easiest ways to burn yourself out before your business can even get off the ground is to try to master everything yourself, and do it all. No matter how good you are, it simply is not realistic. That is where the development of a logical and workable business system comes into play.

Outsourcing as a Way of Systemizing Your Business

Unless you have unlimited funds, chances are you cannot hire a number of full-time employees to handle many of your essential functions. One great way for a small business to have all the efficiency of a larger corporation is to outsource functions when, and as, necessary. There are several important advantages to this approach, especially when money is tight:

- There is a good chance you will pay only a fraction of what it would cost to keep someone on the payroll, plus you don't have to worry about benefits.
- One flat fee per month is much easier to budget and is likely to provide you with all the services you need for any given area, such as Tech Support or Accounting.
- You don't have to buy software, computers, or other office equipment; your outsourcing partners will already have those in place.

The Sky's The Limit

You may be surprised at the range of functions you can effectively outsource. For example, you can outsource:

- **Composition of ad copy and sales collateral.** There are a number of freelance writers with a business background that can easily come up with text for ads and electronic brochures, introductory emails, and even create letter templates that you can use in your business.
- **Accounting.** Freelancers can take on the task of managing your books, including calculating the amount of taxes you owe on monthly revenues and making sure your vendors are paid on time.
- **Customer Support.** There are freelance services that will conduct customer satisfaction surveys, handle inbound customer concerns, and also provide basic information about your product line to interested parties. Some of these services even offer support 24/7, which may be important if you are going for an international clientele.
- **Marketing campaigns.** Freelancers who specialize in marketing can get to know what you do, where you want to take the company, and help you determine what markets to target and create a marketing campaign that is sure to get you the right kind of attention.

- **Systems Support and Troubleshooting.** When your website is down or your online credit card payment program is not functioning properly, you need help now rather than later. A local service that manages computer systems for small businesses may be just what you need. Most will charge a flat fee per month that will cover most routine problems, as well as provide a schedule for any issue that is not covered under the agreement.

The Meaning of Outsourcing/Virtual Assistants

You may have heard the term virtual assistant and outsourcing somewhere by someone in recent years. In the last few years, the terms has been most associated with the situations where companies decided it would be cheaper for them to send a lot of their work overseas so they wouldn't have to pay so much money on labor, since this is the biggest expense for any company. There is a huge controversy over the subject in this regard. Some companies claim they need to do it to save on expenses, especially when the economy begins to flatten out. But there are also arguments against it, where people claim that sending jobs overseas means a loss of employment for those within the states.

But outsourcing does not always equate to jobs being sent overseas. Often, this just means that the work is being contracted outside of the company, instead of hiring hourly or salaried employees to fill those positions. In this sense, it is not only done within the United Sites, but it can even be done locally.

Outsourcing is usually done because the company does not have anyone who has the skills or experience to perform a task well enough to do it right, they don't have enough work to employ someone fulltime, or because of various financial benefits. So the company outsources the job to someone or a company that does have the ability to get the work done properly.

One of the most popular business responsibilities that gets outsourced is payroll. Before outsourcing started, payroll was done in-house. But today, most payroll duties are outsourced to companies like ADP or PAYCHEX.

Speaking of payroll, most small businesses do not use payroll anymore. They have no need to, since they outsource most, if not all, of their workload. In fact, you can outsource all of your accounting for as little as $10 a month. Just $10, and you never have to open a bill or write another check. Everything is automated for you. So, smart companies, instead of hiring employees, use vendors. This is simply a matter of writing a check and giving it to the vendor. It is known as nonemployee compensation.

Let's say you decide to start an online business. You don't have to worry about hiring employees. Just outsource everything. By doing this, you are able to get the business running faster. It also makes running the business easier. And you can create a business that is more profitable than if you hired employees. What you are doing, in a way, is creating what is referred to as a "virtual company."

> The vision is really about empowering workers, giving them all the information about what's going on so they can do a lot more than they've done in the past.
>
> *– Bill Gates, cofounder of Microsoft, richest man in the world*

Why Outsource?

You may ask why you should outsource. The best answer to this question is to save money. But to give further answers, you have to look at it economically.

- Head count changes. What if you had a situation where you did not need so many people to do a job anymore? Instead of firing employees constantly, just outsource what you need, and when you have to change the workload, either end the outsourcing, or alter how many people you need to outsource the work to.

- Lower costs. From financial and economic points of view, you need to lower costs to drive up profits, especially when times are tough.
- Lower the amount you invest. By outsourcing, you can actually lower your investment costs. Simply rent instead of owning everything.
- You may want to stay focused on the big picture; by outsourcing, this gives you leeway to do so.
- You may lack the money to pay employees' wages and benefits.
- From an economic standpoint, outsourcing makes sense. With the money you pay out for outsourcing, you can get double the help at less cost.

What Type of Projects are Outsourced?

Companies hire contractors all the time to perform various tasks. For example, if the company hired a landscaping firm to come one day a week, this could be looked at as outsourcing. Nowadays, you can outsource just about any type of project. The question remains, what parts of your business will you outsource, and who will you give the business to? The following is a quick list of possible duties and projects that can be outsourced:

- Phone calls
- Email management
- Accounting
- Research
- Follow-up
- Websites/blogs/social media/SEO
- Mailing
- Writing/publishing
- Anything that is repetitive.

What are shown above are just a few suggestions to get you started. There are so many more that cannot be listed here.

So, who does outsourcing today? If you did some research, you may find that large companies, including well-known companies, don't have a ton of employees. They outsource much of the work. They find companies that can handle the workload and get the job done better, faster, and cheaper than the employees they have in-house.

You are not confined to local outsourcing, either. If your business is located in New Jersey, for instance, and you found a company in Las Vegas that can do the work for half the cost, it would only make sense for you to engage that company to do the work. Whether the companies are in India, Malaysia, or the Ukraine, you can find cheap labor. You just need to do some research and know who to contact. (I have some great resources for you at the end of this chapter.)

In fact, if you call technical support of many major technology companies, you may just find the person answering the phone is from India or another foreign country. Many IT, accounting, supply chain management, logistics, benefits administration, and sales are typically outsourced.

Other kinds of jobs that may be outsourced can also include the following:

- <u>Creating software and testing</u>: If you know what type of software you want to create, you can outsource the job to a programmer, who can do the creation and testing for you.
- <u>Website design, hosting, analytics, and maintenance</u>: If you are looking to place your website online, and you don't know HTML, no need to fret. Just simply outsource the work. You may be able to find a company that will not only create your web pages for you, but will also host your site, perform analytics, run stats, and even keep your website maintained - all for very low cost.
- <u>Online Marketing</u>: The basics of online marketing consist of writing articles that are formatted for SEO. Plus, there is also signing up for pay-per-click service. You could cheaply outsource your marketing work to other companies and they would do the work for you. For instance, they might do SEO searches, banner placements, text-link placements, and so much more. Plus, if you get a good marketing company, they will be able to work with you, and recommend the type of advertising that would work best.

- <u>Writing and Publishing</u>: If you are looking to have content produced for your website, create e-books to sell to customers, or to provide free content for signing up for your newsletter, but you can't write, just outsource the work. If you are looking to have a book published or some other material printed for advertisements, you can just outsource the printing.

- <u>Customer Service</u>: Everyone knows that customer service gets outsourced all the time. India is the main place where customer service centers are located. This is obvious when you call one and you get someone who talks with an Indian accent.

- <u>Call Centers</u>: Call centers can be outsourced as well. Some call centers deal with customer issues for free, while others charge. No matter how you handle the calls, outsourcing can free you to do other important tasks.

- <u>Fulfillment Centers</u>: One of the biggest problems with online businesses that sell a lot of goods and other merchandise is finding a place to hold the merchandise. Storage space can be costly. Why not just outsource the job to a company that not only provides shipping and receiving, but can handle inventory and drop-shipping when required?

- <u>Research and Development</u>: Many companies have R&D departments. These companies pay large amounts for research to create new products. Instead of paying a high price, these companies can lower their cost by outsourcing R&D to other companies, and thereby saving millions of dollars a year in the process.

The first rule of any technology used in a business is that automation applied to an efficient operation will magnify the efficiency. The second is that automation applied to an inefficient operation will magnify the inefficiency.

–Bill Gates

Finding Outsourcers

There are many ways to find outsource companies. Just go to the Web and look. Two of the top places to find companies for outsourcing are Elance (www.elance.com) and Guru (www.guru.com). They've been around for some time. They happen to be the largest marketplaces to find companies looking for work. All you have to do is post a project, and wait for people to respond with bids. Then, hire the service provider you believe can do the work for the best price.

Elance is the largest site on the Internet, if you go by dollar volume. There are thousands of companies registered on the service. If you have a project to get done, you are sure to find someone on Elance who can do it for you within the price range you want. Search for "virtual assistant" or "personal assistant." Elance's main headquarters are in Mountain View, CA.

Guru has the largest subscriber base per volume. Guru is better than Elance in a number of ways. It is a more comprehensive system that gets involved in transactions more fully, and makes sure all transactions are completed. You will also find the feedback system is more advanced than on Elance. Guru also has substantially more members than Elance. Guru's main headquarters are in Pittsburgh, Pa.

While Elance is focused on mid to large businesses, Guru is geared to getting individual professionals together with small businesses.

Also check out these great sites:

- www.Rentacoder.com
- www.Getafreelancer.com
- www.Sologig.com

If you want overseas workers, you can check out www.yourmaninindia.com ($6.25 per hour). They handle both personal and business tasks, and can work with you in real time. They will oftentimes get work done while you are sleeping. If

English fluency is important to you, make sure to ask the company for the VA (virtual assistant) to take an English test. Always interview your VA before assigning any tasks.

Managing the Outsourcers

I personally like to use a service that is very cheap and allows me to keep track of everything, and to which my outsourcers have daily access. This allows me to manage everything by email. Virtual, remember? Check out www.bizpadz.com.

Working with Outsource Companies

When you do find someone to outsource your work to, you will want to know how best to deal with the company. You deal with it like you do with any other business. You hire the company to do your project, ask to be kept updated on the work's progress, get the project completed on time, and then pay for a finished product.

Although hiring an outsourcing company will take away the risks involved in dealing with employees, there are still risks to consider. But you won't have to worry about doing background checks, payroll, finding employee workspace, or buying equipment for employee use.

Clarity is Key

When hiring outsourcers, you will have to be sure to give clear and consistent instructions to them, so they know and understand exactly what they are required to do. If there is a problem, you have to be available and respond quickly when needed. You will have to make sure there are resources available for them, if required, and have the resources available on a consistent basis. One of the most important components is paying them when the project has been completed. This cannot be stressed enough. In the past, there have been companies who took advantage of the companies they outsourced their work to. Do not do this. You will get a bad reputation for doing so.

When working with outsourcing companies, be practical with them when you do your negotiations. Make sure you express to them the amount of money you are looking to spend. Let them know how long the company is to work on the project and when you expect delivery.

> As to the methods there may be millions and then some, but principles are few. The man who grasps principles can successfully select his own methods. The man who tries methods, ignoring principles, is sure to have trouble.
>
> *–Ralph Waldo Emerson*

Be Generous, Be Serious

You are already saving up to 80% on labor, so don't haggle with them regarding the price. Give them your price and let them do what you hired them to do.

If the outsourcing company should hand you a contract, based on their experience in handling your type of project, check it out with a lawyer, especially if you cannot read the language.

Also, when looking at a contract, look out for a few items that may be important to know. These items are as follows:

- If you spot a term on the contract that goes something like this: "Service level agreement," this is actually the guarantee or warranty you get as part of working with them. Make sure you understand what this term means.
- Another term most often seen in contracts is "Work for hire." Any time there is something to be delivered, there should be a clause in the contract that states that once you pay for it, you own it. That is what the work for hire term signifies.
- You may also see a term on the contract that reads like this: "Resources management." This is not always on contracts, but if it is, you need to know what it means. In most cases, a project needs a team in order for the project to be completed correctly and on time. When you see that term in the contract,

make sure to find out how that works with the company you are working with. If the outsourcing company uses another company to perform certain duties, you need to know that.

- One other term you may find is "Term and termination," which simply refers to how long the contract will last (the "term") and what is needed in order to terminate the contract early (the "termination"). You better fully understand these, especially if you are considering canceling the contract.

An Example of Outsourcing a Job

To help you better understand what I'm talking about, here is an example of a project that a company outsourced to another company. For the sake of this example, I will call the company coming up with the idea Company A.

Company A is a technology company. They only have a few employees. The company wants to expand operations, but needs a programmer to create a tool to help them automate the process. The unfortunate problem is that the company has very few staff members with the time to perform the operations for the project.

You are the head of the technology department. Your task is to find a way around this, while getting the project completed within three weeks on a specific budget. You write down what is required to get the project completed. You list all the steps needed. After you've compiled everything together, it is time to find a way to get the project done.

Your next step is to get on the Internet to find companies that specialize in what you need done. Since you know your project requires programming, you post the details of the job on www.Rentacoder.com, as well as www.ScriptLance.com. Next, you remember you established an account with Elance and Guru before, so you go to these places and also post your project there.

You log in the next day to www.Elance.com and find a number of bids have come in. You review all bids. You go to www.Guru.com, www.Rentacoder.com, and www.ScriptLance.com. You notice very few bids on these boards, except for www.Rentacoder.com, which has about half a dozen.

You decide to take about two days to go through the bids. You finally decide, after much deliberation, to go with a service provider on Elance. You award the project to the service provider, and you get the entire project back within a week, complete and fully functional. You pay the service provider.

You now have your completed project and you are successfully able to institute your company program, which works like a charm. What you have just experienced was outsourcing the project to a third party and working with the company to assure the project got done on time and within budget. You are happy and the company you work for is happy. You go back to Elance and leave feedback for the service provider. Plus, your company gives you a bonus for getting the job done ahead of time and on budget.

This is how outsourcing works. There is nothing to it. Just come up with an idea, know what you want, know the money you need to spend, and know where to look for help.

If you would like more information on outsourcing using virtual assistants, I have a free book and audio from a high-level coaching call where I helped my client create a Standard Operating Procedures (SOP) manual. Just visit me online for your free copy at www.outsourcemylifenow.com. For a free audio CD about how to implement virtual assistants into your business, please visit www.outsourcemylifenow.com.

Tools and Resources

Determine Your Market Size

- Standard Rate and Data Services (www.srds.com)
  This provides annual listings of magazine and customer mailing lists available for rent. Look at the size of the mailing lists. You can usually find print versions available at your local library as well as online.
- NextMark (www.nextmark.com)
  This is a simple online mailing list finder and resource. You can find mailing lists for rent (including email lists) for almost any industry you can think of.

- Overture (www.overture.com)
  Search inventory at discount prices. Use the keyword suggestion tool for better searches.

Locating Manufacturing or Products for Resale

- Thomas's Register of Manufacturers (www.thomasnet.com)
  Searchable database of contract manufacturers for all types of products.
- Drop Shipping (www.dropshipsource.com)
  Get a how-to guide for finding manufacturers that are willing to drop ship directly to your customers. Their directory represents millions of top-level wholesale products from thousands of certified drop shippers and bulk wholesalers that you can use for your online store or auctions. These are the same suppliers used by big retail stores around the country.

Recording Phone & Video Interviews

- Hot Recorder (www.hotrecorder.com)
- Audacity (www.audacity.com)
- Skype (www.swkype.com)
  - Great for interviews, screen sharing and training.
- Pamela for Skype (www.pamela.biz/en/)
  - Great for making video recordings of your Skype interviews or training calls.

Instant Expert Status

- ProfNet (www.prleads.com)
  Get daily leads from journalists looking for experts that they can quote and interview to be used by local outlets and national outlets like CNN, The New York Times, MSNBC and more.
- ExpertClick (www.expertclick.com)
  Connecting experts with the news media. Direct via e-mail to top journalists. Google News feed. Search

Optimized News Releases. Send press releases to 12,000 journalists. More than 5 million hits per month.

- Public Insight Network (www.publicinsightnetwork.org/) Some of your ideas end up in stories on air, in print or online. Nothing you share here is ever published without your explicit permission. Create the great stories that make you value the news.

End-to-End Site Solutions Including Payment Processing

- eBay Store (www.pages.ebay.com/storefronts/start.html) Fees as low as $15 per month, plus eBay fees.
- Yahoo! Store (www.smallbusiness.yahoo.com/ecomerce) Fees as low as $40 per month plus 1.5% per transaction. Includes 24/7 customer support.

Payment Processing Services

- PayPal Cart (www.paypal.com/; see "merchant") Accept credit cards without applying for your own merchant account. No monthly fees.
- Google Checkout (www.checlout.google.com/sell) Requires your customer to have a Google ID.

Cheap Toll-Free Numbers

- Onebox (www.onebox.com) Calls to your toll-free number can be forwarded to any other number.
- Unitel Voice (www.unitelvoice.com) Prices as low as 2.7 cents per minute.

Competitive Website Analysis

- Alexa (www.alexa.com Spy on your competitor's website traffic, ads and keywords.
- Spyfu (www.spyfu.com)

Lots of statistics on what is working for your competitors.

Virtual Receptionist

- Angel (www.angel.com)
  Provides you with an 800 number with professional voice menu in just five minutes.
- Ring Central (www.ringcentral.com)
  You can get toll-free numbers, call screening, call forwarding, voicemail, fax etc. – all online. I use this one.

Order Taking Call Centers (charge per minute)

These centers are useful for taking orders, lead generation and more when you don't need trained salespeople who are trained to overcome objections.

- LiveOps (www.liveops.com)
  Primarily home-based reps with lower charges than most.
- West Teleservices (www.west.com)
  Has a resource employee base of 29,000 worldwide. Used by high-volume and low-volume players alike.

Call Centers That "Close the Sale"

Operators are trained in "closing" and are commissioned. They are focused on closing your sale. This service is primarily for inbound calls for more information, trial offers, and free samples. Best for offers without a price. Fees are higher but can be worth it.

- West Corporation (www.west.com)
  Has script writers, consultants, and in-house trainers.
- Protocol Marketing (www.protocolmarketing.com)
- Triton Technology (www.tritontechnology.com)

CHAPTER 10

THE FINAL WORD

I want to thank you very much for taking the time to read this book and hope that you got a lot out of it. Countless hours of research have gone into this book, as well as direct experience in working with hundreds of clients around the country. Getting credit and cash for your business is easier and faster today than ever before.

I hope this book has enlightened you, surprised you and maybe, even more importantly, motivated and inspired you. If you are truly serious about finally tasting the fruits of independence; being your own boss at last, and not having to take negative comments from anyone anymore; finally being the master of your own destiny, instead of wondering what the future may hold in a job that could be snatched away at any moment - then I invite you to take the next step toward freedom and a true measure of happiness. Get credit and cash for your business and do it the Guerrilla way.

Now that I've given you an entire toolbox full of tools, it's time for you to take the next step, which is to go and make things happen. You have nothing to lose by trying the techniques in this book; in fact you have everything to gain. You're now well prepared to go and grow your business and live your dreams.

Shameless Plug

From time to time, we have clients that just come and tell us they want trade credit and cash lines of credit, but they do not want to make any personal guarantees and, most importantly, they want someone else to do all the work for them. Well, if you fall into this category, then we have a solution for you. We do have a program that is done-4-you. It is expensive because it is all handled by attorneys, but you can rest

assured it is done right and done fast. Just visit our website at
www.simplybusinesscredit.com and click on the Done-4-You button to
get more info.

In closing, I want you to know that I have faith in you, and know
that if you simply follow what I have covered in this book, then you
will be successful. Please visit our website at www.simplybusiness
credit.com and let us know of your experiences.

Let Me Know Your Victories!

By using this new knowledge that you have, it now becomes
power. You can access money on demand, achieve the dreams that you
never thought were possible, and live the life that you've always
wanted. I know you can do it and I even want to hear about it. Tell me
about your successes; send me an email. I know that you want to share
your success stories. Let me share what you're doing and what's worked
for you with others around the country.

In closing, I'd like to leave you with some inspirational words from
a commencement speech given at Stanford University in 2005 by Steve
Jobs, the late creative genius and CEO behind Apple Computer, who
also happened to be a college dropout:

> "For the past 33 years, I have looked in the mirror every
> morning and asked myself: 'If today were the last day of my
> life, would I want to do what I am about to do today?' And
> whenever the answer has been 'no' for too many days in a row,
> I know I need to change something … almost everything – all
> external expectations, all pride, all fear of embarrassment or
> failure – these things just fall away in the face of death, leaving
> only what is truly important. Remembering that you are going
> to die is the best way I know to avoid the trap of thinking you
> have something to lose."

I couldn't have said it better. My wish for you is to live your life to
the fullest, build or grow your business, and pass it on by leaving a
legacy to your children so that they can learn from you.

You only have one life. Now go out there and live it.

RESOURCES
&
APPENDIX

Common Questions

Question: "My credit is in the dumps right now. Can I use my new business funds to pay off my debts and pay them at a discount?"

Answer: Yes! Our debt settlement course teaches you how to negotiate 40% to 80% discounts on your own personal debt, which is a good way to use your new business funds. For business owners, it's often true that much of your personal debt comes from business expenses anyway. Using business credit to satisfy those debts is often simply a matter of appropriating the debt where it should have been in the first place. By using the business cash lines of credit to pay off the personal debt, you transfer the debt from the personal side to the business side, so now it's completely out of your personal name. Our program also provides you with the added bonus of being able to pay it off at a tremendous discount. You can learn more about our course by visiting us online at www.simplybusinesscredit.com.

Question: "I just want to clean up my credit. Will your system help me?"

Answer: Actually, I think that's selling yourself a bit short because if you want to clean up your credit, no problem, we can help you do that; but think about it this way: most credit repair places will say, "Yeah, we can get a mark removed off your credit," and you say, "Oh cool, now I don't have to pay it."

But you *do* still have to pay it. They're still going to hound you. They're still going to come after you, even after you have bad credit. You don't want that. So we help you get out of that cycle. Our debt settlement course enables you to settle that debt at a 40% to 80% discount, so that it's taken care of and gone forever. You can learn more about our course by visiting us online at www.simplybusinesscredit.com.

Question: What is the real difference between business and personal credit?

Answer: The real difference is that business credit will not be showing up on your personal credit report. If you have business credit and it is showing up on your personal credit report, then it really is not business credit after all, is it? I see this often when people think they are getting a business credit card. When it arrives, it shows up on their personal credit report. It is really just a personal card with a business name on it. So, how do you overcome this drawback?

The system outlined in this book and on my website will teach you how to get real business credit by using your tax ID number. Notice that I say "system," meaning that there are a series of steps that need to be done in order to get to this point. In the book, I give you a step-by-step guide for you to be able to do this yourself over the course of several years. Or, you can opt into our "done-4-you" option to considerably cut down on the amount of time it takes to secure these valuable lines of business credit. You can learn more about what we offer at www.simplybusinesscredit.com.

Question: Do I need to have good personal credit to get business credit?

Answer: If you are building credit under your businesses' name and following the process set forth in this book, then your personal credit won't matter at all! However, if you fail to follow these prescribed steps, and you are only able to build credit under your name, then yes – you will need good personal credit.

But our system teaches you how to get business credit whether you have good credit or not. Getting business credit is like the old saying about making your first million. Making your first million is always the hardest. The second one is much easier. Once you do it the first time, you just repeat the process over and over again to make more money. The same is true for achieving success with business credit.

Obviously, the better your credit score from the start, the faster this process will be able to be done. I have found that if you have at least a 680 credit score, your chances of accelerating this process increase. However, if this is not the case, then simply follow the sections of this book on debt settlement and credit repair, and your success will be right around the corner. You can also visit our website at www.simplybusinesscredit.com to see how we may be able to customize our services to meet your needs.

Question: What can I do to improve my Personal Credit Rating?

Answer: First, everyone who is going through this process needs to have an updated copy of his or her credit report with his or her current credit score. Remember, they change all the time, due to several factors. I offer a service that can do amazing things for your credit in just 90 days. If you have bad credit, I recommend that you start here while you are building your corporate file. To find out more about this program, please visit our website at www.simplybusinesscredit.com.

Question: What if I have a bankruptcy on my credit report?

Answer: When it comes to bankruptcy, this is the most accurate data we have in terms of clearing it up before the standard period of 10 years expires. There's a 60% chance that you can get it removed from your credit report before the full 10 years is up. This is a surprise to most people, but it's true. It is the same statistic with foreclosures. However, you will not be able to remove foreclosures, bankruptcies and tax liens yourself. You will need the help of an attorney. For more information, you can visit our website at www.simplybusinesscredit.com.

Question: What about removing late payments that appear on your credit report?

Answer: Late payments are pretty easy to remove. With my new program, they have become super easy to remove. You have to understand that when you apply for personal credit, you need to read the fine print on the terms of agreement. Some agreements are written in a way that allow the lender to report your payment as 30, 60, or 90 days late, even if you are only one or two days late. However, you can actually use this clause against the lender in order to remove late payments from your credit report. Let's say for example that you were actually 40 days late. If the fine print states the late payment is reported that you are 30 days late, you may be able to remove this since, technically, you were late, but not within the 30 days as the document states.

For more information on how to make this work for you, you can visit our website at www.simplybusinesscredit.com.

Personal Credit Reporting Agencies

1. TransUnion.
   P.O. Box 2000, Chester, PA 19022-2000
   1-800-916-8800
   www.transunion.com
2. Experian
   P.O. Box 2104, Allen, TX 75013
   1-888-397-3742
   www.experian.com
3. Equifax
   P.O. Box 740241, Atlanta, GA 30374
   1-800-685-1111
   www.equifax.com

Business Credit Reporting Agencies

1. **Dun & Bradstreet (D&B)**
D&B is the primary business credit reporting agency with over 70 million businesses registered in their database. A business credit file with D&B contains information provided by the business owner and vendors of the business. D&B issues a PAYDEX score based on payment experiences and a DUNS rating based on financials. Its business credit builder program is a great way for business owners to add trade references to their file in a short period of time.

2. **Equifax Small Business Enterprise**
Small **Business Equifax**, one of the three primary consumer credit reporting agencies, also provides business credit evaluations for over 22,000,000 small businesses and corporations.

3. **Experian SmartBusinessReportsTM**
Experian Business is another one of the three primary consumer credit reporting agencies who provides business credit evaluations as well. SmartBusinessReports assigns a business credit score called the Intelliscore.

4. **FDInsight™**
This is a company that is relatively new to the business credit market. It was originally the second largest credit reporting company in the mortgage broker field. The information on their business files is provided by the business owner or a third party, and then every piece of information is verified by the staff of FDInsight™. They are known to provide the most accurate business credit report in the industry.

5. **Credit.net**
Credit.net is a division of InfoUSA® that generates credit reports on approximately 15,000,000 businesses. The credit analysis provided by Credit.net relies on four criteria: years in business, number of employees, public records, and stability within the industry. Its business credit score is a grading system from A through C (70-100) and is awarded as an evaluation of the company's credit history.

6. **Accurint® Business**

This is a new business that is a combination of forces between The Better Business Bureau (BBB) and LexisNexis. Accurint Business is like **Business Experian** in that they provide public and business profile information, including credit history based on payment patterns of small, medium, and large companies.

7. **ClientChecker**

This is a **business credit bureau** that started in 2003 and specifically targets small businesses, freelance professionals, and contractors searching for information to help them determine which other businesses they should do business with. Rather than providing a fixed business credit score, ClientChecker compiles information based on feedback from its members.

8. **Paynet**

Paynet collects real-time loan information from more than 200 leading U.S. lenders. The company's database has a collection of commercial loans and leases. It's the largest proprietary database of long-term debt over a period of 10 years.

9. **Cortera**

Cortera provides credit information on businesses large and small but then combines it with ratings from a community of small business owners, who provide feedback both good and bad on these businesses.

10. **ChexSystems**

The tenth reporting agency is extremely important, as it has to do with your ability to open up a business checking account with a financial institution. Banks use a reporting agency known as ChexSystems, which is a network comprised of member Financial Institutions that regularly contribute information on mishandled checking and savings accounts to a central location.

Debt Statute of Limitation

	Oral	Written	Promissory	Open
Alabama	6	6	6	3
Alaska	6	6	3	3
Arizona	3	6	6	3
Arkansas	6	6	3	3
California	2	4	4	4
Colorado	6	6	6	6
Connecticut	3	6	6	3
Delaware	3	3	3	4
Florida	4	5	5	4
Georgia	4	6	6	4
Hawaii	6	6	6	6
Idaho	4	5	5	4
Illinois	5	10	10	5
Indiana	6	10	10	6
Iowa	5	10	5	5
Kansas	3	6	5	3
Kentucky	5	15	15	5
Louisiana	10	10	10	3
Maine	6	6	6	6
Maryland	3	3	6	3
Massachusetts	6	6	6	6
Michigan	6	6	6	6
Minnesota	6	6	6	6

Mississippi	3	3	3	3
Missouri	5	10	10	5
Montana	5	8	8	5
Nebraska	4	5	5	4
Nevada	4	6	3	4
New Hampshire	3	3	6	3
New Jersey	6	6	6	6
New Mexico	4	6	6	4
New York	6	6	6	6
North Carolina	3	3	5	3
North Dakota	6	6	6	6
Ohio	6	15	15	6
Oklahoma	3	5	5	3
Oregon	6	6	6	6
Pennsylvania	4	4	4	4
Rhode Island	15	15	10	10
South Carolina	3	3	3	3
South Dakota	3	6	6	6
Tennessee	6	6	6	6
Texas	4	4	4	4
Utah	4	6	6	4
Vermont	6	6	5	3
Virginia	3	5	6	3
Washington	3	6	6	3
West Virginia	5	10	6	5
Wisconsin	6	6	10	6
Wyoming	8	10	10	8

Statute of Limitations That Are Revived or Extended Only By a Written New Promise to Pay:
(Debtor sending a payment does not revive or extend statute of limitations.)

State	Code Section
Arizona	12-508
California	CCP 360
Colorado	13-80-113
Florida	5.4
Iowa	614.11
Kansas	60-250
Maine	14-860
Massachusetts	260-13
Michigan	27A.5866
Minnesota	541.17
Mississippi	15-1-73
Missouri	516.320
Nevada	11.390
New York	GOL 17-101
Texas	16.065
West Virginia	55-2-8
Wisconsin	893.45

Review of Websites Mentioned

Personal Credit Reports

1. TransUnion.
   P.O. Box 2000, Chester, PA 19022-2000
   1-800-916-8800
   www.transunion.com
2. Experian
   P.O. Box 2104, Allen, TX 75013
   1-888-397-3742
   www.experian.com
3. Equifax
   P.O. Box 740241, Atlanta, GA 303743
   1-800-685-1111
   www.equifax.com
4. Free Reports for Military
   www.SaveandInvest.org/military

Free Money

- www.gov.benefits.gov.
- www.grants.gov.
- www.grants.gov/appsets/GDG_AppUserGuide_0207.pdf.
- www.foundationcenter.org/getstarted/individuals/
- www.fundsnetservices.com.

Federal Money Programs

- www.Grants.gov
- www.ed.gov/about/offices/list/ocfo/grants/grants.html
- www.grantsolutions.gov
- www.grants.gov/assets/GDG_AppUserGuide_0207.pdf
- www.sba.gov
- www.fsa.usda.gov
- www.dla.cmil.db
- www.rurdev.usda.gov
- www.sba.gov/INV/venture.html
- www.foundationcenter.com/getstarted/individuals/
- www.Fundsnetservices.com
- www.womensnet.net

- www.ehome-basedbusiness.com/articles/
- www.dressforsuccess.org
- www.fns.usda.gov/cnd/lunch or
  www.fns.usda.gov/fdd/programs/nsip
- www.idanetwork.org
- www.adea.org
- www.aoa.org
- www.helpingpatients.org
- www.hud.gov/offices/
- www.hud.gov/office/cpd/affordablehousing/programs/home/ad di
- www.ftc.gov
- www.ed.gov/about/offices/list/fsa/index.html
- www.ed.gov/about/offices/list/ope/iegps/index.html
- www.ed.gov/programs/iegpsirs/index.html
- www.studentaid.ed.gov
- www.rankinfoundation.org
- www.aauw.org/fga/fellowships_grants/
- www.grants.nih.gov/grants/index.cfm
- www.ed.gov/about/offices/list/ocfo/grants/grants
- www.spencer.org/programs/grants/research_grants.htm
- www.energystar.gov
- www.hud.gov/economicdevelopment/index.cfm
- www.taxcreditcompany.com
- www.ntctac.com
- www.firstgov.gov
- www.pueblo.gsa.gov/call
- www.rurdev.usda.gov
- www.staff.lib.msu.edu/harris23/grants/3women.htm
- www.govbenefits.gov
- www.dla.mil/db
- www.fsa.usda.gov
- www.osdbuweb.gov
- www.sba.gov/INV/venture.html
- www.sba.gov/aboutsba/sbaprograms/inv/index.html
- www.sba.gov/aboutsba/sbaprograms/onlinewbc/index.html
- www.schoolgrants.org

Outsourcings Tools & Resources
- www.Elence.com
- www.Odesk.com
- www.Guru.com
- www.yourmaninindia.com/
- www.Rentacoder.com
- www.Getafreelancer.com
- www.Sologig.com

Manage Outsourcers
- www.Bizpadz.com
- www.Basecamp.com

Determine Your Market Size
- Standard Rate and Data Services (www.srds.com)
- NextMark (www.nextmark.com)
- Overture (www.overture.com)

Locating Manufacturing or Products for Resale
- Thomas's Register of Manufacturers (www.thomasnet.com)
- Drop Shipping (www.dropshipsource.com)

Recording Phone & Video Interviews
- Hot Recorder (www.hotrecorder.com)
- Audacity (www.audacity.com)
- Skype (www.swkype.com)
- Pamela for Skype (www.pamela.biz/en/)

Instant Expert Status
- ProfNet (www.prleads.com)
- ExpertClick (www.expertclick.com)
- Public Insight Network (www.publicinsightnetwork.org/)

End-to-End Site Solutions Including Payment Processing
- eBay Store (www.pages.ebay.com/storefronts/start.html)
- Yahoo Store (www.smallbusiness.yahoo.com/ecomerce)

Payment Processing Services

- PayPal Cart (www.paypal.com; see "merchant")
- Google Checkout (www.checlout.google.com/sell)

Cheap Toll-Free Numbers

- Onebox (www.onebox.com)
- Unitel Voice (www.unitelvoice.com)

Competitive Website Analysis

- Alexa (www.alexa.com)
- Spyfu (www.spyfu.com)

Corporate Credit Reports

1. Dun & Bradstreet (D&B)
2. Equifax Small Business Enterprise
3. Experian SmartBusinessReportsTM
4. FDInsight™
5. Credit.net
6. AccurintTMBusiness
7. ClientChecker
8. Paynet
9. Cortera
10. ChexSystems

Different Forms of Business:

In order from least to most complicated

Sole Proprietorship

A sole proprietorship is the simplest form of a business. This means that you are the sole owner – the buck stops there.

If you own a sole proprietorship, you will need to fill out a Schedule C federal income tax form when you do your yearly taxes. On this schedule, you will be asked to list your income from the business, and will be given the opportunity to claim business deductions. Certain deductions, such as depreciation and the use of an office in the home, require you to fill out separate tax forms, then enter their totals on the appropriate Schedule C lines.

When you're finished with your schedule C, you'll have an amount that represents your annual net income for that business. You'll be instructed to enter this amount on the front side of your 1040 form. This amount is added in with other income to give you your total income, which, after deducting certain other items, becomes your total taxable income. As a sole proprietor, you'll also be required to pay self-employment tax on the net income from your home business. This is derived by a convoluted formula, but works out to be about 13% or 14% of your business profits. This is a hefty chunk of change which, for many taxpayers, amounts to a larger amount than they pay for their federal taxable income liability.

Advantages

- Little to no bureaucratic red tape involved
- Least expensive to set up
- Tax? You and the business are the same
- Business losses will offset gains from other income sources

Disadvantages

- All responsibility for everything rests on your shoulders

170

• For liability purposes, you and the company are the same

This is a very important thing to consider. For instance, as the sole proprietor, if you face a reversal of fortune because of ill health or some other unforeseeable circumstance, your creditors will still have rights to your money.

If you sell your business assets and still cannot pay your personal assets, such as your home or your car, your personal savings, retirement savings, or all of these things may be in jeopardy.

The same liability applies to your personal assets should someone sue you or your company for any reason. If you lose, all of your personal assets and property could be forfeited.

Partnerships

Partnerships fall between sole proprietorships and corporations (but closer to sole proprietorships) in terms of complexity and governmental regulations. You can have a legal partnership without even writing up articles of partnership, though it's unwise to do so. All you basically need to do to launch this type of business is apply for any required business permits and start operations.

Although most home businesses are "one-person shops," it is not uncommon to find those that have two or more partners, including people who live together and those that do not. Partnerships share several characteristics, including the unlimited liability of at least one of the partners, the co-ownership of assets by the partners, the limited life of the partnership, mutual agency, and share of management and profits.

The definition of a partnership, according to The Uniform Partnership Act (which has been adopted by many states), is "an association of two or more persons to carry on as co-owners of a business for profit." Let's take a look at two types of partnerships:

1. General Partnership
2. Limited Partnership

General Partnership

This is where two or more people are decision-making owners in the business.

Advantages

- The General partnership is pretty simple.
- You and your partners are equals, sharing equally in the management and the profits.
- You have the benefit of your partners' financial resources, skills and abilities instead of just your own.
- No one new can join the partnership without permission of all the partners.
- You don't need a contract between you and your partners, but one is advisable.

Disadvantages

- You will also share all financial responsibility – even if one of the partners signs a $500,000 contract on behalf of the company after you gave explicit instructions not to!
- Your personal assets are still in jeopardy should the company incur liability in any way.
- Each partner is taxed on his share, whether or not the money was distributed during the year.

Limited Partnership

In this arrangement, there are two kinds of partners, General and Limited. The General Partner has the same advantages and disadvantages as in a General Partnership.

The Limited Partner is more like a stockholder. His liability is limited to his investment in the business. However, this partner <u>cannot</u> be involved in the management of the company. If he does get involved, he loses his immunity from personal liability.

172

Limited Partnerships are normally formed in conjunction with real estate companies for tax advantages.

Advantages

- Allows access to additional financing through the partners.
- Can have general partners as well as limited partners, thereby gaining advantages of both forms of business.

Disadvantages

- There is a lot of additional paperwork involved.
- The state keeps a very sharp eye on this kind of business.
- As a general partner you still have all the disadvantages of a general partnership.

Partnerships are not taxed on their income. Instead, the income (or losses) "pass through" to the individual partners and are taxed as income to them.

This is similar to the way things are handled in a sole proprietorship, except that additional tax forms must be filed at tax time. While more tax forms must be completed for a partnership than for a sole proprietorship, the amount of extra paperwork for a partnership is nowhere near as much as is required for corporations.

Partners must show their partnership income as personal income on form 1040 when completing their annual tax returns. They must also pay self-employment taxes on this income. Like the other business structures, the partnership can offset its income by allowable deductible business expenses.

Corporation

This is by far the most complex of all the business structures. Business owners that form corporations do so generally to take advantage of a major benefit of this type of structure: limitation of liability. The downside of having a corporation is the added burden and expense of regulations and red tape, and in some instances, the double taxation that hits a corporation.

Corporations are typically formed under the authority of a state government. If a corporation does business in more than one state, it is subject to federal interstate commerce laws and to the various laws of the states in which it operates.

Takes Some Planning

Creating a corporation isn't as quick and easy as forming a sole proprietorship or partnership. The procedure usually involves taking subscriptions for capital stock and creating a tentative organization. Approval must then be obtained from the Secretary of State in the state in which the corporation will be formed. The approval comes in the form of a charter, which specifies the powers and limitations of the corporation.

In many ways a corporation is the ideal business form even if your business is very small. Corporations are not necessarily giant companies with offices in many states. They can be tiny companies of one or two people (often referred to as "Closely Held"). Using this business form can be a very smart move on your part.

A Closely Held Corporation does not sell stock like a Public Corporation. It is made up of just a few people (or possibly just yourself alone) who are all involved in the day-to-day running of the business to one degree or another.

Advantages

- Depending on your state of incorporation, you may have as few as one person in your corporation.
- Limited liability. The corporation is separate from you.
- The business continues intact even if the owner dies. Ownership of the company is easily transferred.
- Fewer rules and regulations.

Disadvantages

- More paperwork and bureaucracy involved.
- Personal Collateral may still be necessary to get loans.
- Initial cost of incorporation.

Incorporation fees vary from state to state, however you may always consider incorporating your business in another state, such as Nevada, where the laws favor small businesses. There are many sites on the Internet that can help you form a corporation at the least possible cost. If you don't have Internet access, simply look in the back of the Wall Street Journal or USA Today newspaper.

Be sure to do your homework concerning the requirements of out-of-state corporations doing business in your home state.

You may incorporate in Nevada to save yourself some money only to find that you still have to register your corporation in your home state.

Corporation Types

C-Corporation, also known as a "C-Corp," is started by filing Articles of Incorporation. This is a highly structured business entity and must comply with very specific rules. There are certain corporate formalities that must be observed. The stockholders, officers and directors must treat the business as an independent legal entity, which includes holding regular scheduled meetings, filing corporate papers with the state, and filing a separate corporate tax return. If your goal is to take your company "public" (IPO) and sell shares, this structure is the form to use to reach that goal. One of the advantages of this entity is the greater number of business deductions available with a C-Corp versus an S-Corp. A disadvantage of a C-Corp is double taxation. If the corporation makes a profit for the year, it is taxed. If the corporation passes the profits onto the stockholders in the form of a dividend, then the stockholders are also taxed.

S-Corporation, also known as an "S-Corp," is started by filing Articles of Incorporation. The stockholders file a specific form with the Internal Revenue Service asking that the corporation be taxed as a sole proprietor or partnership. The number of stockholders in an S-Corp is limited to 75, plus all must be citizens of the United States. The advantage of an S-Corp versus a C-Corp is that the profits and losses flow through to the stockholders on their individual tax returns. Only the stockholders pay taxes, not the corporation. Another advantage is that if losses are incurred, they can be passed through to the individual's personal tax return, therefore offsetting, or possibly reducing, their personal income tax.

Limited Liability Company, also called an "LLC", is a good entity to use for small businesses as well as large because it (1) provides the limited liability protection of a corporation, (2) allows the profits and losses to flow through to the members without double taxation, and (3) offers a flexible management structure and allocation of profits and losses. Like a corporation, an LLC offers protection to the owners because they are shielded from personal liability for the business debts or legal claims made against the LLC. The plaintiff (person suing) can only satisfy a judgment from the assets held in the name of the company. Liability protection is critical in this age of unexpected litigation that can wipe out an individual's lifetime of savings.

Corporate Taxation

Because the subject of corporate taxation is far too complex to deal with here, we'll simply say that a corporation is taxed differently than a partnership or a sole proprietorship because the corporate entity itself is taxed on corporate income, and then the shareholders are taxed on the income they receive from their shares in the corporation. In the sole proprietorship and the partnership, the business entities themselves are not taxed.

You can own a corporation and have the corporation hire you as an employee to manage it. The corporation pays you a wage and provides company-paid benefits, such as health insurance. The wages and benefits are tax deductible to the corporation. You pay taxes on the wages you receive. The corporation pays corporate taxes on the profits that remain after paying you for your wages and benefits.

This situation applies to the regular corporation (C-corp), but not to the S-corp. The S-corp is not taxed as a business entity. Rather, the income or losses pass through to the shareholders, where they are taxed as personal income, just as happens in the sole proprietorship and the partnership.

We recommend using an LLC or S-Corp for your corporate structure to build your business credit the fastest. However, this is not legal or accounting advice; it is crucial that you discuss the formation of your business entity with an attorney or tax advisor to determine the best entity to use for your specific situation. If you have previously formed a corporation, now is the perfect time to review with a professional to confirm that you still are using the best type of entity. If not, make the appropriate changes.